A Companion to the Study of the Kitáb-i-Íqán

The Study Companions Series

A Companion to the Study of the Kitáb-i-Íqán

prepared by

Hooper C. Dunbar

George Ronald
Oxford

George Ronald, *Publisher*
46 High Street, Kidlington, Oxford OX5 2DN

© Hooper C. Dunbar 1998
All Rights Reserved

Reprinted 2000

ISBN 0–85398–430–1

Typeset by Stonehaven Press, Knoxville, Tennessee
Printed and bound in Great Britain by Biddles Ltd
www.biddles.co.uk

Contents

. . . all the Scriptures and the mysteries thereof are condensed into this brief account. So much so, that were a person to ponder it a while in his heart, he would discover from all that hath been said the mysteries of the Words of God, and would apprehend the meaning of whatever hath been manifested by that ideal King.

Bahá'u'lláh, *Kitáb-i-Íqán*, p. 237

Introduction

The materials gathered together in this book are intended to stimulate study of Bahá'u'lláh's Book of Certitude, the Kitáb-i-Íqán. With repeated use in classes, they have evolved over a number of years into their present form which, it is hoped, will prove useful for both individual and group study.

In the future undoubtedly whole volumes will be compiled drawing together information of this sort. If, for the present, these notes assist the student of the Íqán to acquire a broader vision of its fundamental themes and truths and prove a convenient point of reference for explanations not always at hand, they will have served their intended purpose.

Whatever help notes of this kind may offer, ultimately, of course, the Íqán speaks for itself. It is its own great expounder. The verses themselves illumine each other and the reader. May eager explorers of the Íqán's luminous expanse be guided by it towards the sublime heights of certitude and positive knowledge which it reveals.

Hooper C. Dunbar
Haifa 1998

A Note from the Publisher

The numbers identifying passages of the Kitáb-i-Íqán refer to paragraphs rather than pages. Future editions of the Íqán will carry such paragraph numbers. A letter of the Universal House of Justice to a National Spiritual Assembly dated 6 April 1995 indicates that the invocation at the beginning of the book 'In the Name of our Lord, the Exalted, the Most High' is not numbered. Numbering begins with the paragraph 'No man shall attain . . .' and continues throughout the book to the final paragraph, number 290. Similarly, numbers identifying passages of the Kitáb-i-Aqdas refer to paragraphs.

For those whose copies of the Kitáb-i-Íqán do not carry the paragraph numbering system, we suggest that each paragraph be numbered by hand to facilitate study of the text.

1

The Importance of the Íqán and its Study

Shoghi Effendi characterizes the Kitáb-i-Íqán as a 'unique repository of inestimable treasures' occupying a position 'of unsurpassed preeminence among the doctrinal . . . writings of the Author of the Bahá'í Dispensation'.[1] The whole of his masterful description is cited in chapter 2. Throughout his ministry Shoghi Effendi, in letters written on his behalf, continually reiterated the importance of the Íqán, the need for its careful study and, indeed, its mastery. A selection of these significant statements follows. Each of them should heighten the interest and quicken the initiative of every would-be student of the Íqán.

> The Sacred Books are full of allusions to this new dispensation. In the 'Book of Íqán', Bahá'u'lláh gives the keynote and explains some of the outstanding passages hoping that the friends will continue to study the Sacred Books by themselves, and unfold the mysteries found therein.[2]

> The Íqán is the most important book written on the spiritual significance of the Cause.[3]

> . . . the Íqán is the most important book wherein Bahá'u'lláh explains the basic beliefs of the Faith . . .[4]

> You should form study classes and read the important books that have been published, especially the 'Íqán', which contains the basic tenets of the Faith. The one who ponders over that book and grasps its full significance will

obtain a clear insight into the old scriptures and appreciate the true Mission of the Báb and Bahá'u'lláh.[5]

Shoghi Effendi hopes that you will exert all your effort to deepen your knowledge of the literature of the Movement, until you become fully acquainted with its spirit and tenets. Unless you do obtain such a firm hold you will never be able to teach others and render real service to the promulgation of the Faith. Of special importance is the Book of the Íqán which explains the attitude of the Cause towards the prophets of God and their mission in the history of society. Besides this there is *Some Answered Questions* of the Master and *The Dawn-Breakers* of Nabíl. Every Bahá'í should master these books and be able to explain their contents to others. Besides their importance, they are interesting and most absorbing.[6]

He fully approves the idea of holding study classes, for the deeper the friends go in their understanding of their teachings the more firm and steadfast they will become and the more unwavering in their support of the institutions of the Faith. Books such as the *Íqán*, *Some Answered Questions* and *The Dawn-Breakers* should be mastered by every Bahá'í. They should read these books over and over again. The first two books will reveal to them the significance of this divine revelation as well as the unity of all the Prophets of old.[7]

. . . it is the most fundamental book on the Bahá'í Revelation.[8]

He is very eager to have this wonderful book translated well, for it is the best means of grounding those who become interested in the fundamental teachings of the Faith. The Íqán and Dr Esslemont's book will be sufficient to make any seeker a true believer in the divine nature of the Faith.[9]

. . . 'the Book of Certitude' by Bahá'u'lláh . . . contains the very essence of the Teachings, and because of its clarity and its relative simplicity can greatly appeal to every

thoughtful reader . . . the Íqán deepens the knowledge of
the reader by acquainting him with some of the basic
theological problems of the Faith. It is, therefore, indis-
pensable for every student of the Movement . . .[10]

He was particularly gratified to learn of your intention
to make a thorough study of the 'Kitáb-i-Íqán' during this
summer . . . The friends, and particularly those who wish
to become competent and useful teachers, should indeed
consider it to be their first duty to acquaint themselves, as
thoroughly as they can, with each and every detail contained in this Holy Book, so that they may be able to
present the Message in a befitting manner.

It is the Guardian's hope, therefore, that those among
the believers who have thus far and for some reason or
another, failed to make a serious study of this important
work will be stimulated to do so, and will as a result
deepen their comprehension of the essentials of the
Faith.[11]

Observations on the Study of the Íqán
and on Scripture in General

The Íqán has been described by Bahá'u'lláh in one of His
Tablets at the World Centre as the 'Siyyid-i-Kutúb' – the
Lord of Books. Any penetration of its inexhaustible meanings obviously requires careful and prolonged effort
in its study. The reading of the scriptures, Bahá'u'lláh
clarifies in the Íqán, 'is for no other purpose except to
enable the reader to apprehend their meaning and unravel
their innermost mysteries. Otherwise reading, without
understanding, is of no abiding profit unto man'.[12] The understanding and comprehension of His words, He further
affirms, are 'in no wise dependent upon human learning.
They depend solely upon purity of heart, chastity of soul,
and freedom of spirit'.[13]

We have already seen above Shoghi Effendi's admoni-
tions to read and re-read this exalted text – indeed, to

master its essential content. In this process we would not feel unduly discouraged if our grasp seems too limited, for the study of this book is a lifetime occupation. True progress in this regard is conditioned upon the progressive unfoldment of one's own inner state:

> The heart must needs therefore be cleansed from the idle sayings of men, and sanctified from every earthly affection, so that it may discover the hidden meaning of divine inspiration, and become the treasury of the mysteries of divine knowledge.[14]

The eminent Bahá'í scholar Mírzá Abu'l-Faḍl recounted to Ali Kuli Khan 'that he had read the Íqán with "the eye of intellect" seventeen times through, and it had seemed to him a meaningless string of words. That later, he had read it with "the eye of faith", and had found it the key with which he could unlock the secrets of all the sacred books of past religions.'[15]

By intensively studying the Íqán we will be responding to Bahá'u'lláh's exhortation to immerse ourselves in the ocean of His words, 'that ye may unravel its secrets, and discover all the pearls of wisdom that lie hid in its depths'.[16] 'Abdu'l-Bahá counsels the student to 'investigate and study the Holy Scriptures word by word so that you may attain knowledge of the mysteries hidden therein. Be not satisfied with words, but seek to understand the spiritual meanings hidden in the heart of the words.'[17] Shoghi Effendi reassuringly affirms that 'the more we read the Words the more will the truth they contain be revealed to us'.[18] Further, he states:

> If you read the utterances of Bahá'u'lláh and 'Abdu'l-Bahá with selflessness and care and concentrate upon them, you will discover truths unknown to you before and will obtain an insight into the problems that have baffled the great thinkers of the world.[19]

One note of caution. The truths of the Íqán are best acquired within the context of its own wholeness and in the light of Bahá'u'lláh's other writings. 'We must never take one sentence in the Teachings and isolate it from the rest . . .'[20] At the same time, 'we cannot divorce the letter from the spirit of the words. As Bahá'u'lláh says we should take the outward significance and superimpose upon it the inner. Either without the other is wrong and defective.'[21]

2

The Significance
and Historical Circumstances
of the Revelation of the Íqán

Shoghi Effendi on the Significance of the Íqán

The following passage from *God Passes By* serves as an ideal introduction to the study of the Íqán. Here Shoghi Effendi broadly characterizes the text of the Íqán in itself and in relation to other works of Bahá'u'lláh, places it in historical context, sets forth the circumstances of its revelation and indicates its fundamental and underlying purpose:

1 Foremost among the priceless treasures cast forth from the
2 billowing ocean of Bahá'u'lláh's Revelation ranks the
3 Kitáb-i-Íqán (Book of Certitude), revealed within the space
4 of two days and two nights, in the closing years of that
5 period (1278 AH/1862 AD). It was written in fulfilment
6 of the prophecy of the Báb, Who had specifically stated
7 that the Promised One would complete the text of the
8 unfinished Persian Bayán, and in reply to the questions
9 addressed to Bahá'u'lláh by the as yet unconverted mater-
10 nal uncle of the Báb, Ḥájí Mírzá Siyyid Muḥammad, while
11 on a visit, with his brother, Ḥájí Mírzá Ḥasan-'Alí, to
12 Karbilá. A model of Persian prose, of a style at once origi-
13 nal, chaste and vigorous, and remarkably lucid, both
14 cogent in argument and matchless in its irresistible elo-
15 quence, this Book, setting forth in outline the Grand
16 Redemptive Scheme of God, occupies a position un-
17 equalled by any work in the entire range of Bahá'í litera-
18 ture, except the Kitáb-i-Aqdas, Bahá'u'lláh's Most Holy
19 Book. Revealed on the eve of the declaration of His Mis-
20 sion, it proffered to mankind the 'Choice Sealed Wine',

21 whose seal is of 'musk', and broke the 'seals' of the 'Book'
22 referred to by Daniel, and disclosed the meaning of the
23 'words' destined to remain 'closed up' till the 'time of the
24 end'.

25   Within a compass of two hundred pages it proclaims
26 unequivocally the existence and oneness of a personal
27 God, unknowable, inaccessible, the source of all Revela-
28 tion, eternal, omniscient, omnipresent and almighty;
29 asserts the relativity of religious truth and the continuity
30 of Divine Revelation; affirms the unity of the Prophets,
31 the universality of their Message, the identity of their
32 fundamental teachings, the sanctity of their scriptures,
33 and the twofold character of their stations; denounces the
34 blindness and perversity of the divines and doctors of
35 every age; cites and elucidates the allegorical passages of
36 the New Testament, the abstruse verses of the Qur'án,
37 and the cryptic Muḥammadan traditions which have bred
38 those age-long misunderstandings, doubts and animosities
39 that have sundered and kept apart the followers of the
40 world's leading religious systems; enumerates the essen-
41 tial prerequisites for the attainment by every true seeker
42 of the object of his quest; demonstrates the validity, the
43 sublimity and significance of the Báb's Revelation; ac-
44 claims the heroism and detachment of His disciples;
45 foreshadows, and prophesies the world-wide triumph of
46 the Revelation promised to the people of the Bayán;
47 upholds the purity and innocence of the Virgin Mary;
48 glorifies the Imáms of the Faith of Muḥammad; celebrates
49 the martyrdom, and lauds the spiritual sovereignty, of the
50 Imám Ḥusayn; unfolds the meaning of such symbolic
51 terms as 'Return', 'Resurrection', 'Seal of the Prophets'
52 and 'Day of Judgement'; adumbrates and distinguishes
53 between the three stages of Divine Revelation; and expati-
54 ates, in glowing terms, upon the glories and wonders of
55 the 'City of God', renewed, at fixed intervals, by the
56 dispensation of Providence, for the guidance, the benefit
57 and salvation of all mankind. Well may it be claimed that
58 of all the books revealed by the Author of the Bahá'í
59 Revelation, this Book alone, by sweeping away the age-
60 long barriers that have so insurmountably separated the
61 great religions of the world, has laid down a broad and
62 unassailable foundation for the complete and permanent
63 reconciliation of their followers.[22]

Notes on This Passage

Lines 3–4 'within the space of two days and two nights'

There are a number of references in the Bahá'í writings to the rapidity with which the Báb and Bahá'u'lláh revealed the divine verses:

> A certain Muḥammad Karím, a native of <u>Sh</u>íráz, who had been a witness to the rapidity and the manner in which the Báb had penned the verses with which He was inspired, has left the following testimony to posterity, after attaining, during those days, the presence of Bahá'u'lláh, and beholding with his own eyes what he himself had considered to be the only proof of the mission of the Promised One: 'I bear witness that the verses revealed by Bahá'u'lláh were superior, in the rapidity with which they were penned, in the ease with which they flowed, in their lucidity, their profundity and sweetness to those which I, myself saw pour from the pen of the Báb when in His presence. Had Bahá'u'lláh no other claim to greatness, this were sufficient, in the eyes of the world and its people, that He produced such verses as have streamed this day from His pen.'[23]

Line 5 '1862 AD'

There are several passages in the Íqán itself which indicate the date of its revelation, such as 'these holy lights have, for eighteen years, heroically endured the showers of afflictions'.[24] Add eighteen to the beginning of the Bahá'í Era in 1844. In the lunar calendar the Íqán was revealed in 1278 AH and the Bahá'í Faith was founded in 1260 AH, eighteen years earlier.

Lines 4–5 'that period'

The period under review in this passage refers to the Ba<u>gh</u>dád period, particularly the six years following the return of Bahá'u'lláh from His two-year retirement in Kurdistan (1856–63). The Íqán was revealed during the time Bahá'u'lláh resided in 'an extremely modest residence', which He later designated as 'The Most Great House' – 'His "Most Holy Habitation", out of which had "gone forth the breath of the All-Glorious", and from which had poured forth, in "ceaseless strains", the "melody of the All-Merciful"'.[25] It is this House which Bahá'u'lláh has ordained as a centre of pilgrimage.[26]

Line 6 'the prophecy of the Báb'

The Báb specified that the 'Bayán' is not completed and that 'He Whom God would manifest' (Bahá'u'lláh) would complete it, though not in its actual form, but only spiritually in the form of another book. The 'Íqán' is believed to be its continuation.[27]

Lines 7–8 'the unfinished Persian Bayán'

Shoghi Effendi refers to the Persian Bayán thus:

Peerless among the doctrinal works of the Founder of the Bábí Dispensation; consisting of nine Váḥids (Unities) of nineteen chapters each, except the last Váḥid comprising only ten chapters . . . this Book, of about eight thousand verses, occupying a pivotal position in Bábí literature, should be regarded primarily as a eulogy of the Promised One rather than a code of laws and ordinances designed to be a permanent guide to future generations.[28]

The Báb Himself comments on the position of the Bayán in relation to the revelation of the Promised One:

I swear by the most holy Essence of God – exalted and glorified be He – that in the Day of the appearance of Him Whom God shall make manifest a thousand perusals of the Bayán cannot equal the perusal of a single verse to be revealed by Him Whom God shall make manifest

. . . And know thou of a certainty that every letter revealed in the Bayán is solely intended to evoke submission unto Him Whom God shall make manifest, for it is He Who hath revealed the Bayán prior to His Own manifestation.[29]

Lines 9–10 'maternal uncle of the Báb'

Ḥájí Mírzá Siyyid Muḥammad, one of the three brothers of Fáṭimih Bagum, the mother of the Báb. (For further details concerning the uncles of the Báb, see below 'The Uncles of the Báb'.) It is interesting to note that because of its recipient the Íqán was originally known as 'Risáliy-i-Khál' or 'Treatise to the Uncle'. Bahá'u'lláh Himself later renamed it the Kitáb-i-Íqán.

Lines 20–1 '"Choice Sealed Wine" whose seal is of "musk"'

Reference to the Qur'án, Surih 83:25–6: 'Choice Sealed Wine must be given them to quaff, the seal of musk . . .' According to various Muslim commentators, this refers to the wine drunk by the righteous in Paradise. Its vessels are said to be sealed with musk instead of clay.

A number of passages from Bahá'u'lláh's Tablets refer to this choice sealed wine. For example:

Verily I say, the seal of the Choice Wine hath, in the name of Him Who is the Self-Subsisting, been broken; withhold not thyself therefrom.[30]

By the righteousness of God! Idle fancies have debarred men from the Horizon of Certitude, and vain imaginings withheld them from the Choice Sealed Wine.[31]

Similarly, in His Most Holy Book Bahá'u'lláh states:

> Think not that We have revealed unto you a mere code of
> laws. Nay, rather, We have unsealed the choice Wine with
> the fingers of might and power.[32]

The significance attributed to this spiritual wine in contrast
to 'the wine that men drink' is unfolded by Bahá'u'lláh
thus:

> Fear ye God, O people of the earth, and think not that the
> wine We have mentioned in Our Tablets is the wine which
> men drink, and which causeth their intelligence to pass
> away, their human nature to be perverted, their light to
> be changed, and their purity to be soiled. Our intention
> is indeed that wine which intensifieth man's love for God,
> for His Chosen Ones and for His loved ones, and igniteth
> in the hearts the fire of God and love for Him, and glorifi-
> cation and praise of Him. So potent is this wine that a drop
> thereof will attract him who drinketh it to the court of His
> sanctity and nearness, and will enable him to attain the
> presence of God, the King, the Glorious, the Most Beaute-
> ous. It is a wine that blotteth out from the hearts of the
> true lovers all suggestions of limitation, establisheth the
> truth of the signs of His oneness and divine unity, and
> leadeth them to the Tabernacle of the Well-Beloved, in the
> presence of God, the Sovereign Lord, the Self-Subsisting,
> the All-Forgiving, the All-Generous. We meant by this
> Wine, the River of God, and His favour, the fountain of
> His living waters, and the Mystic Wine and its divine grace,
> even as it was revealed in the Qur'án, if ye are of those
> who understand. He said, and how true is His utterance:
> 'A wine delectable to those who drink it.' And He had no
> purpose in this but the wine we have mentioned to you,
> O people of certitude![33]

Line 21 'and broke the "seals" of the "Book"'

> But thou, O Daniel, shut up the words, and seal the book,
> [even] to the time of the end . . .[34]

Line 22–4 'disclosed the meaning of the "words" destined to remain "closed up" till the "time of the end"'

And he said, Go thy way, Daniel: for the words [are] closed up and sealed till the time of the end.[35]

Line 25 'two hundred pages'

This is the length of the original Persian manuscript copy in 'Abdu'l-Bahá's calligraphy.

Lines 26–7 'a personal God'

What is meant by personal God is a God Who is conscious of His creation, Who has a Mind, a Will, a Purpose, and not, as many scientists and materialists believe, an unconscious and determined force operating in the universe. Such conception of the Divine Being, as the Supreme and ever present Reality in the world, is not anthropomorphic, for it transcends all human limitations and forms, and does by no means attempt to define the essence of Divinity which is obviously beyond any human comprehension. To say that God is a personal Reality does not mean that He has a physical form, or does in any way resemble a human being. To entertain such belief would be sheer blasphemy.[36]

Line 29 'the relativity of religious truth and the continuity of Divine Revelation'

This is the fundamental principle which 'constitutes the bedrock of Bahá'í belief'.[37] It is summarized by Shoghi Effendi:

The fundamental principle enunciated by Bahá'u'lláh . . . is that religious truth is not absolute but relative, that Divine Revelation is a continuous and progressive process, that all the great religions of the world are divine in origin, that their basic principles are in complete harmony, that their aims and purposes are one and the same, that their teachings are but facets of one truth, that their functions are complementary, that they differ only in the nonessential aspects of their doctrines, and that their missions represent successive stages in the spiritual evolution of human society.[38]

Lines 51–7

Notes commenting on the specific topics found in these lines are incorporated into chapter 5, 'Annotations to the Íqán'.

Lines 58–9 'of all the books revealed by the Author of the Bahá'í Revelation'

Bahá'u'lláh's many writings fill, in the words of Shoghi Effendi, a hundred volumes:

. . . volumes replete with unnumbered exhortations, revolutionizing principles, world-shaping laws and ordinances, dire warnings and portentous prophecies, with soul-uplifting prayers and meditations, illuminating commentaries and interpretations, impassioned discourses and homilies, all interspersed with either addresses or references to kings, to emperors and to ministers, of both the East and the West, to ecclesiastics of divers denominations, and to leaders in the intellectual, political, literary, mystical, commercial and humanitarian spheres of human activity.[39]

Lines 60–1 'the great religions of the world'

In a letter written on his behalf Shoghi Effendi stated that the Bahá'í Revelation

constitutes the ninth in the line of existing religions, the latest and fullest Revelation which mankind has ever known. The eighth is the religion of the Báb and the remaining seven are: Hinduism, Buddhism, Zoroastrian-

ism, Judaism, Christianity, Islám, and the religion of the
Sabaeans. These religions are not the only true religions
that have appeared in the world but are the only ones still
existing. There have always been Divine Prophets and
Messengers, to many of whom the Qur'án refers. But the
only ones existing are those mentioned above.[40]

Circumstances of the Revelation of the Íqán

Regarding Shí'í Islám

A basic understanding of Islám, and particularly of Shí'í
Islám, which for centuries has prevailed in Bahá'u'lláh's
native land of Iran, helps open the way for the Western
reader to more fully appreciate many of the references
found in the Íqán. It is useful to remember that the recipient of the book was, himself, of Shí'í persuasion. The
following extract from a work written by William Hatcher
and Douglas Martin provides a brief introduction to such
an understanding:

> Like Christianity before it, Islam gradually divided into
> a number of major sects. One of the most significant of
> these is the Shiah sect, which believes that it was Muham-
> mad's intention that his descendants inherit the spiritual
> and temporal leadership of the faithful. These chosen
> ones, called Imams, or 'leaders', were believed to be
> endowed with unqualified infallibility in the discharge of
> their related responsibilities. However, the great majority
> of Muslims rejected such claims believing that the *sunna*
> – the 'way' or mode of conduct attributed by tradition to
> the Prophet Muhammad – was a sufficient guide. Those
> who subscribed to this latter belief became known as
> Sunni. Although Sunni Muslims vastly outnumber the
> Shiah today, and are usually referred to by Western schol-
> ars as 'orthodox' as opposed to the 'heterodoxy' of the
> Shiah, Shiah Islam has a long and respected tradition, a
> tradition that only recently has become the object of

serious study among a growing group of non-Muslim scholars.

By 661 AD, only twenty-nine years after Muhammad's death, power in the Muslim world fell into the hands of the first of a series of dynastic rulers, theoretically elected by the faithful, but in fact representing the dominance of various powerful families. The first two of these Sunni dynasties, the Umayyads and the Abbasids, saw the Imams as a challenge to their own legitimacy. Consequently, according to Shiah accounts, one Imam after another was put to death, beginning with Hasan and Husayn, grandsons of Muhammad. These Imams, or descendants of the Prophet, came in time to be regarded by Shiah Islam as saints and martyrs.

Although Shiah Islam began among the Arabs, it reached its greatest influence in Persia. From the beginning, the Persian converts to Islam were attracted by the idea of the Imam as a divinely appointed leader. Unlike the Arabs, the Persians possessed a long heritage of government by a divinely appointed monarch, and the devotion that gathered around this figure in time came to focus on the person of the Prophet's descendants and appointed successors. After centuries of oppression by Sunni caliphs, the tradition of the Imamate eventually triumphed in Persia, through the rise of a strongly Shiah dynasty, the Safavids. in the sixteenth century.

By this time, however, the line of Imams had ended. One of the features of Iranian Shiah tradition is that, in the year 873, the twelfth and last appointed Imam – only a child at the time – withdrew into 'concealment' in order to escape the fate of his predecessors. It is believed that he will emerge 'at the time of the end' to usher in a reign of justice throughout the world . . . Among other titles Muslims have assigned to this promised deliverer, the 'Hidden Imam', are *Mahdi* (the Guided One) and *Qá'im* (He Who Will Arise – i.e. from the family of the Prophet).

For a period of sixty-nine years following his disappearance, the twelfth or Hidden Imam was said to have communicated with his followers through a series of deputies. The intermediaries took the title *báb* (gate), because they were the only way to the Hidden Imam. There had been four bábs up to the year 941, when the fourth one died without naming a successor.

   The refusal of either the Imam or the final báb to name a successor implied that the matter was to be left by the faithful entirely in the hands of God. In time, a messenger or messengers of God would appear, one of whom would be the Imam Mahdi, or Qá'im, and who would again provide a direct channel for the Divine Will to human affairs. It was out of this tradition that the Bahá'í religion and its forerunner, the Bábí Faith, appeared in the mid-nineteenth century.[41]

The Uncles of the Báb

Fáṭimih Bagum, the mother of the Báb, had three brothers, all of whom figure in Bahá'í history.

ḤÁjí Mírzá Siyyid 'Alí

Khál-i-A'ẓam, the Greatest Uncle, characterized by Shoghi Effendi as 'noble and serene'.[42] He was one of the leading merchants of Shíráz.

   It was this same uncle into whose custody the Báb, after the death of His father, was entrusted, and who, on his Nephew's return from His pilgrimage to Hijáz and His arrest by Ḥusayn Khán, assumed undivided responsibility for Him by pledging his word in writing. It was he who surrounded Him, while under his care, with unfailing solicitude, who served Him with such devotion, and who acted as intermediary between Him and the hosts of His followers who flocked to Shíráz to see Him.[43]

He eventually offered up his life as one of the renowned Seven Martyrs of Ṭihrán.

ḤÁjí Mírzá Siyyid Muḥammad

Khál-i-Akbar, the Greater Uncle (also referred to as Khál-i-Aṣghar), the eldest of the uncles. He engaged in business with the Báb in Búshihr. Unconverted in the ministry of the Báb, he later travelled to Iraq where he called on Bahá'u'lláh and became the honoured recipient of the Íqán. The revelation of this book in answer to his questions was followed by his private acceptance of the Faith, an acceptance which eventually became clearly known through his open affirmations of the fact in his will and testament.

ḤÁJÍ MÍRZÁ ḤASAN-'ALÍ

Khál-i-Asghar, the Younger Uncle, also a merchant engaged with the Báb in trade. He journeyed with Khál-i-Akbar on his trip to Iraq to visit the Shí'í holy places but adamantly refused to accompany him to see Bahá'u'lláh. Later in his life, however, he also embraced the new Faith.

Extracts from Two Historical Accounts

The following two accounts, one by Hand of the Cause Hasan Balyuzi and the other by Adib Taherzadeh, provide further important narrative information related to the circumstances surrounding the writing of the Íqán.

> The Kitáb-i-Íqán or *The Book of Certitude* was written in answer to questions presented by Ḥájí Mírzá Siyyid Muḥammad, a maternal uncle of the Báb, entitled Khál-i-Akbar (the Greatest Uncle). He and his brother, Ḥájí Mírzá Ḥasan-'Alí, entitled Khál-i-Asghar (the Younger or the Junior Uncle) were visiting the holy shrines of 'Iráq, in the year 1862. Both of them, during the six short eventful years of the ministry of their Nephew, had stood firm and steadfast in His support and defence, but neither of them had given Him his allegiance. Bahá'u'lláh, Himself, relates in a Tablet that Ḥájí Siyyid Javád-i-Karbilá'í spoke to Him of the presence of these two uncles of the Báb in 'Iráq. Bahá'u'lláh then enquired from Ḥájí Siyyid Javád whether he had reminded them of the Cause of the Báb. Ḥájí Siyyid Javád had not, and Bahá'u'lláh related

in the Tablet that He wished such close relatives of the Primal Point not to remain deprived of the bounties conferred by the Faith of their glorious Nephew, and He directed Ḥájí Siyyid Javád to bring one or both of them to meet Him. Already in Shíráz Ḥájí Mírzá Siyyid Muḥammad had been prompted by a relative, Áqá Mírzá Áqá, Núri'd-Dín, to travel to 'Iráq, outwardly on pilgrimage to the holy shrines, but in truth with the aim of attaining the presence of Bahá'u'lláh. (As a youth, Áqá Mírzá Áqá had been converted to the Bábí Faith by his aunt, Khadijih Bigum, the wife of the Báb.) Now, when Ḥájí Siyyid Javád-i-Karbilá'í, whom he had known well for many years, brought Ḥájí Mírzá Siyyid Muḥammad this invitation from Bahá'u'lláh, he gladly and readily responded. Bahá'u'lláh mentions in the same Tablet that when He asked Ḥájí Mírzá Siyyid Muḥammad what it was that stood in his way, the latter replied that there were some questions which had caused him great concern. Bahá'u'lláh advised him to write down those questions that they might be answered. In recent years, amongst the papers left by Ḥájí Mírzá Siyyid Muḥammad, the questions he presented to Bahá'u'lláh have come to light. These, which we can read today in the handwriting of Ḥájí Mírzá Siyyid Muḥammad himself, are related to the Shí'ih expectations of the advent of the Qá'im of the House of Muḥammad.

Ḥájí Mírzá Siyyid Muḥammad worded his questions under four headings, namely:

1. The Day of Resurrection. Is there to be corporeal resurrection? The world is replete with injustice. How are the just to be requited and the unjust punished?

2. The twelfth Imám was born at a certain time and lives on. There are traditions, all supporting the belief. How can this be explained?

3. Interpretation of holy texts. This Cause does not seem to conform with beliefs held throughout the years. One cannot ignore the literal meaning of holy texts and scripture. How can this be explained?

4. Certain events, according to the traditions that have come down from the Imáms, must occur at the advent of the Qá'im. Some of these are mentioned. But none of these has happened. How can this be explained?

This is the gist of the questions presented to Bahá'u'lláh, by the uncle of the Báb.[44]

Ḥájí Mírzá Siyyid Muḥammad was so affected by meeting Bahá'u'lláh that he immediately wrote a letter to his son, Ḥájí Mírzá Muḥammad-Taqí, in which he said:

'. . . I attained the presence of His Honour Bahá' (may peace be upon Him) and I wish you could have been present! He treated me with the utmost affection and favour and graciously asked me to stay for the night. It is an absolute truth that deprivation from His bounteous presence is a grievous loss. May God bestow upon me the privilege of attaining His presence perpetually . . .'

The Kitáb-i-Íqán dispelled every doubt that Ḥájí Mírzá Siyyid Muḥammad had harboured in his mind. As a result of reading this book he reached the stage of certitude and recognized the station of the Báb. In his will, written some years later, he declared his faith, acknowledged the authenticity of the Messages of the Báb and Bahá'u'lláh and identified himself as a follower of these twin Manifestations of God.[45]

Concerning the Original Manuscript of the Íqán

The three following extracts contain various facts regarding the history and fate of the original manuscript copy of the Íqán given to Ḥájí Mírzá Muḥammad. The third passage, penned by the Hand of the Cause Dr Ugo Giachery, offers an intimate view of Shoghi Effendi's own attitude towards this priceless heritage.

The original copy of the *Kitáb-i-Íqán*, which Ḥájí Mírzá

Muḥammad received, was transcribed by 'Abdu'l-Bahá Who was then eighteen years of age. In the margins of a few pages Bahá'u'lláh has, in His own hand, made some corrections and towards the end of the book has written this passage:

> Amidst them all, We stand, life in hand, wholly resigned to His will; that perchance, through God's loving kindness and His grace, this revealed and manifest Letter may lay down His life as a sacrifice in the path of the Primal Point, the most exalted Word. By Him at Whose bidding the Spirit hath spoken, but for this yearning of Our soul, We would not, for one moment, have tarried any longer in this city. 'Sufficient Witness is God unto Us.'

For many years this original copy of the *Kitáb-i-Íqán* remained with the family of Ḥájí Mírzá Siyyid Muḥammad, until in 1948 his great-granddaughter Fáṭimih Khánum-i-Afnán presented it to Shoghi Effendi, the Guardian of the Faith. It reached him a few years later and was placed in the Bahá'í International Archives Building on Mount Carmel, Haifa.[46]

Bahá'u'lláh revealed the *Kitáb-i-Íqán*, answering the questions posed by this uncle of the Báb, within forty-eight hours. The original manuscript, in the handwriting of 'Abdu'l-Bahá, with marginal additions made by Bahá'u'lláh Himself, is now preserved in the International Bahá'í Archives on Mount Carmel.

Fáṭimih Khánum Afnán, a great-granddaughter of Ḥájí Mírzá Siyyid Muḥammad, had inherited this manuscript and she presented it to the Guardian of the Bahá'í Faith. A copy, which must have been transcribed for Ḥájí Mírzá Ḥasan-'Alí, the junior uncle of the Báb (who, although he did not accompany his brother into the presence of Bahá'u'lláh, before long gave Him his allegiance), bears a date only one year after its revelation; it is now in the possession of one of Ḥájí Mírzá Ḥasan-'Alí's great-great-grandsons . . .

The Book of Certitude was perhaps the earliest of the

Writings of Bahá'u'lláh to appear in print. A beautifully lithographed copy, which does not bear a date and must have been printed in Bombay, is known to have been in circulation in the early eighties of the last century.[47]

. . . I should like to mention an episode which further demonstrates the eager interest of Shoghi Effendi in collecting information and facts pertaining to the Sacred Writings and the history of the Cause. One evening, as I entered the dining-room, the Guardian was already seated at his place at the table, his face shining with an inner jubilation which he could neither control nor conceal. At his side, upon the table, stood a small bundle, an object wrapped in a coloured silk handkerchief, typical of the East and of Írán in particular. As soon as we were all seated and attentive, even before dinner was served, he said that a pilgrim had that day arrived from Ṭihrán, bringing with him one of the most precious documents to be placed in the archives. He untied the handkerchief and with great reverence lifted out a manuscript in book form, and, placing it in a position that every one could see, added that it contained two original Tablets in the handwriting of 'Abdu'l-Bahá. One was the *Íqán* and the other was a Tablet the name of which I do not now remember.

These manuscripts, Shoghi Effendi stated, were transcribed by 'Abdu'l-Bahá in His beautiful calligraphy, when He was about eighteen years old, and bore some additions in the Hand of Bahá'u'lláh, insertions which He had written on the margins of many pages in reviewing the manuscripts. Shoghi Effendi had never before seen the original of the *Íqán* and was deeply astonished to discover that the phrase he had chosen from this book and placed on the title page of his translation of Nabíl's Narrative, *The Dawn-Breakers*, was an after-reflection of Bahá'u'lláh's, written by Himself, on the margin of one page. The phrase in question is the one starting: 'I stand, life in hand, ready; that perchance . . .'

The Guardian, that evening, was not only astonished but overjoyed as well, because he was conscious that through a mysterious process he had been inspired to adopt that phrase as an eternal testimonial to Bahá'u'lláh's yearning to sacrifice His life for the Báb, the Primal Point.

All of us who were seated at the table were awed and profoundly stirred, and I, in particular, felt that the existence of a spiritual link between our Guardian and the invisible world of God was something that no one should ever doubt.[48]

Translations of the Íqán

The following list of translations of the Book of Certitude offers further evidence of its progressive international influence. Within 140 years of its revelation, renderings have been made in 36 languages, most of them published in several editions and revisions. Shoghi Effendi produced his masterful English rendering of the Íqán in 1931 and thereafter it became the standard for translations into other languages.

Afrikaans	1985	Esperanto	(manuscript)
Albanian	1932	French	1904, 1965
Arabic	1934	German	*circa* 1930, 1958
Armenian	(manuscript)	Greek	1992
Bengali	1975	Gujarati	(manuscript)
Bulgarian	1995	Icelandic	1994
Burmese	(manuscript)	Indonesian	1997
Chinese	*circa* 1932, 1982	Italian	1955
Czech	(manuscript)	Japanese	1977
Danish	1974	Kurdish	(manuscript)
Dutch/Flemish	1937	Latvian	1995
English	1904, 1931	Norwegian	(manuscript)
English Braille	1935	Portuguese	1957

Romanian	1991	Swedish	1936
Russian	1933, 1994	Tongan	1991
Serbian	(manuscript)	Turkish	1969
Shona	1986	Urdu	1914, 1955
Spanish	1937	Xhosa	1979

3

Major Themes of the Íqán
Identified by Shoghi Effendi

Summary of Themes taken from *God Passes By*, p. 139

This review of the contents of the Íqán as set forth by Shoghi Effendi is here broken down point by point and is correlated with individual paragraphs of the text. Principal references are indicated in bold. One way to study the Íqán is to copy out these themes without the paragraph references, read through the Íqán and make your own set of references which can then be compared with the following list.

1) Proclaims unequivocally the existence and
   oneness of a personal God   19, 100, **104**, 190

   • Unknowable   56, 98, **104–5**, 224

   • Inaccessible   56, 150

   • Source of all Revelation   53, 106, 149, 155

   • Eternal   10, 16, 147, 196

   • Omniscient   84, 104, 182

   • Omnipresent   55, 109, 149, 197

- the abstruse verses of the Qur'án
  36, 46, 49–51, 57, 75, 80, 83–4, 86–7,
  92–5, 121, 129, 148, 186, 188, 194–6,
  209–11, 224–31, 234–8, **283**

- and the cryptic Muḥammadan traditions
  33–4, 38–40, 86, 172, **201–2**,
  204, 266–75 *passim*, **281–4**

which have bred those age-long misunderstandings,
doubts and animosities that have sundered and kept
apart the followers of the world's leading religious
systems.

6) Enumerates the essential prerequisites for the
attainment by every true seeker of the object of
his quest   1–2, 77, 128, **213–16**, 233

7) Demonstrates the validity, the sublimity and
significance of the Báb's Revelation   256–63

8) Acclaims the heroism and detachment of His
disciples   84, 163–4, 170, 247–9, 263–4

9) Foreshadows, and prophesies the world-wide
triumph of the Revelation promised to the
people of the Bayán   84–5, 101, 219

10) Upholds the purity and innocence of the Virgin
Mary   59

11) Glorifies the Imáms of the Faith of Muḥammad
33, 38, 113, 152, 161

12) Celebrates the martyrdom, and lauds the
spiritual sovereignty, of the Imám Ḥusayn
135–40

13) Unfolds the meaning of such symbolic terms as

- 'Return'   156, **160–71**, 180, 217

- 'Resurrection'   51, 114, **123–5, 152–3,**
                                        160, 163–9, **182**

- 'Seal of the Prophets'
                    172, 174, 178–82, 196, 237

- 'Day of Judgement'
                    51, 114, 118, 121, **122–4,** 128, 186

14) Adumbrates and distinguishes between the
    three stages of Divine Revelation
                    107, 109, **149–51,** 182

15) Expatiates, in glowing terms, upon the glories
    and wonders of the 'City of God', renewed, at
    fixed intervals, by the dispensation of Provi-
    dence, for the guidance, the benefit and
    salvation of all mankind   **217–19**

The following is a breakdown of these themes as
numbered above for the parts of the Íqán:

Part One: Themes   1, 2, 3, 4, 5, 8, 10, 11, 13

Part Two: Themes   1, 2, 3, 4, 5, 6, 7, 8, 9, 11, 12,
                     13, 14, 15

Extracts from the Íqán Cited by Shoghi Effendi in *The Dispensation of Bahá'u'lláh*

In 1934 Shoghi Effendi penned his powerful exposition of the essential verities of the Bahá'í Faith, *The Dispensation of Bahá'u'lláh*. In it he cited, in support of his argument, a number of excerpts from the Íqán related to God and His Manifestations. These convey not only the most basic Bahá'í doctrines but the essence of the message of the Íqán. As such, they should be thoroughly considered and assimilated. The numbers in brackets refer to paragraphs in the Íqán.

On God, the Unknowable Essence

He Who in unnumbered passages claimed His utterance to be the 'Voice of Divinity, the Call of God Himself' thus solemnly affirms in the Kitáb-i-Íqán: 'To every discerning and illumined heart it is evident that God, the unknowable Essence, the Divine Being, is immeasurably exalted beyond every human attribute such as corporeal existence, ascent and descent, egress and regress . . . He is, and hath ever been, veiled in the ancient eternity of His Essence, and will remain in His Reality everlastingly hidden from the sight of men . . . He standeth exalted beyond and above all separation and union, all proximity and remoteness . . .' [104] 'God was alone; there was none else beside Him' is a sure testimony of this truth. [105][49]

On the Appearance of God's Prophets

'The door of the knowledge of the Ancient of Days', Bahá'u'lláh further states in the Kitáb-i-Íqán, 'being thus closed in the face of all beings, He, the Source of infinite grace . . . hath caused those luminous Gems of Holiness to appear out of the realm of the spirit, in the noble form of the human temple, and be made manifest unto all men, that they may impart unto the world the mysteries of the unchangeable Being and tell of the subtleties of His imperishable Essence . . . [106] All the Prophets of God, His well-favoured, His holy and chosen Messengers are, without exception, the bearers of His names and the embodiments of His attributes . . . [110] These Tabernacles of Holiness, these primal Mirrors which reflect the Light of unfading glory, are but expressions of Him Who is the Invisible of the Invisibles.'[109][50]

On the Power and Sovereignty of the Prophets

'They Who are the Luminaries of Truth and the Mirrors reflecting the light of Divine Unity,' Bahá'u'lláh explains in the Kitáb-i-Íqán, 'in whatever age and cycle they are sent down from their invisible habitations of ancient glory unto this world to educate the souls of men and endue with grace all created things, are invariably endowed with an all-compelling power and invested with invincible sovereignty . . . [103] These sanctified Mirrors, these Day-Springs of ancient glory are one and all the exponents on earth of Him Who is the central Orb of the universe, its essence and ultimate purpose. From Him proceed their knowledge and power; from Him is derived their sovereignty. The beauty of their countenance is but a reflection of His image, and their revelation a sign of His deathless glory . . . Through them is transmitted a grace that is infinite, and by them is revealed the light that can never fade . . . [106] Human tongue can never befittingly sing their praise, and human speech can never unfold their mystery.' [109][51]

On the Unity of the Prophets

'Inasmuch as these Birds of the celestial Throne', He adds, 'are all sent down from the heaven of the Will of God, and as they all arise to proclaim His irresistible Faith, they therefore are regarded as one soul and the same person . . . [161] They all abide in the same tabernacle, soar in the same heaven, are seated upon the same throne, utter the same speech, and proclaim the same Faith . . . [162] They only differ in the intensity of their revelation and the comparative potency of their light . . . That a certain attribute of God hath not been outwardly manifested by these Essences of Detachment doth in no wise imply that they Who are the Day-Springs of God's attributes and the Treasuries of His holy names did not actually possess it.' [111]⁵²

On the Continuity of Divine Revelation

'To believe that all revelation is ended, that the portals of Divine mercy are closed, that from the daysprings of eternal holiness no sun shall rise again, that the ocean of everlasting bounty is forever stilled, and that out of the tabernacle of ancient glory the Messengers of God have ceased to be made manifest' [148] must constitute in the eyes of every follower of the Faith a grave, an inexcusable departure from one of its most cherished and fundamental principles.⁵³

Passages from the Íqán Selected by Shoghi Effendi for Inclusion in *Gleanings from the Writings of Bahá'u'lláh*

Shoghi Effendi selected twenty-four passages from the Íqán and arranged them in six sections in *Gleanings from the Writings of Bahá'u'lláh*. In this sense they may be considered his compilation of key portions of the book and as such should be carefully noted. The paragraph locations in the Íqán are added in square brackets after each passage cited.

Gleanings, Section XIII, pp. 17–27

Consider the past. How many, both high and low, have, at all times, yearningly awaited the advent of the Manifestations of God in the sanctified persons of His chosen Ones. How often have they expected His coming, how frequently have they prayed that the breeze of Divine mercy might blow, and the promised Beauty step forth from behind the veil of concealment, and be made manifest to all the world. And whensoever the portals of grace did open, and the clouds of divine bounty did rain upon mankind, and the light of the Unseen did shine above the horizon of celestial might, they all denied Him, and turned away from His face – the face of God Himself . . . [3]

Reflect, what could have been the motive for such deeds? What could have prompted such behaviour towards the Revealers of the beauty of the All-Glorious? Whatever in days gone by hath been the cause of the denial and opposition of those people hath now led to the perversity of the people of this age. To maintain that the testimony of Providence was incomplete, that it hath therefore been the cause of the denial of the people, is but open blasphemy. How far from the grace of the All-Bountiful and from His loving providence and tender mercies it is to single out a soul from amongst all men for the guidance of His creatures, and, on one hand, to withhold from Him the full measure of His divine testimony, and, on the other, inflict severe retribution on His people for having turned away from His chosen One! Nay, the manifold bounties of the Lord of all beings have, at all times, through the Manifestations of His Divine Essence, encompassed the earth and all that dwell therein. Not for a moment hath His grace been withheld, nor have the showers of His loving-kindness ceased to rain upon mankind. Consequently, such behaviour can be attributed to naught save the petty-mindedness of such souls as tread the valley of arrogance and pride, are lost in the wilds of remoteness, walk in the ways of their idle fancy, and follow the dictates of the leaders of their faith. Their chief concern is mere opposition; their sole desire is to ignore the truth. Unto every discerning observer it is evident and manifest that had these people in the days of each of the Manifestations of the Sun of Truth sanctified their eyes, their ears, and their hearts from whatever they had seen, heard, and felt, they surely would not have been deprived of beholding the beauty of God, nor strayed far from the habitations of glory. But having weighed the testimony of God by the standard of their own knowledge, gleaned from the teachings of the leaders of their faith, and found it at variance with their limited understanding, they arose to perpetrate such unseemly acts . . . [14]

Consider Moses! Armed with the rod of celestial domin-

ion, adorned with the white hand of Divine knowledge,
and proceeding from the Párán of the love of God, and
wielding the serpent of power and everlasting majesty, He
shone forth from the Sinai of light upon the world.
He summoned all the peoples and kindreds of the earth
to the kingdom of eternity, and invited them to partake
of the fruit of the tree of faithfulness. Surely you are aware
of the fierce opposition of Pharaoh and his people, and of
the stones of idle fancy which the hands of infidels cast
upon that blessed Tree. So much so that Pharaoh and his
people finally arose and exerted their utmost endeavour
to extinguish with the waters of falsehood and denial the
fire of that sacred Tree, oblivious of the truth that no
earthly water can quench the flames of Divine wisdom, nor
mortal blasts extinguish the lamp of everlasting dominion.
Nay, rather, such water cannot but intensify the burning
of the flame, and such blasts cannot but ensure the preservation of the lamp, were ye to observe with the eye of
discernment, and walk in the way of God's holy will and
pleasure . . . [12]

And when the days of Moses were ended, and the light
of Jesus, shining forth from the Day Spring of the Spirit,
encompassed the world, all the people of Israel arose in
protest against Him. They clamoured that He Whose
advent the Bible had foretold must needs promulgate and
fulfil the laws of Moses, whereas this youthful Nazarene,
who laid claim to the station of the divine Messiah, had
annulled the laws of divorce and of the sabbath day – the
most weighty of all the laws of Moses. Moreover, what of
the signs of the Manifestation yet to come? These people
of Israel are even unto the present day still expecting that
Manifestation which the Bible hath foretold! How many
Manifestations of Holiness, how many Revealers of the
light everlasting, have appeared since the time of Moses,
and yet Israel, wrapt in the densest veils of satanic fancy
and false imaginings, is still expectant that the idol of her
own handiwork will appear with such signs as she herself
hath conceived! Thus hath God laid hold of them for their
sins, hath extinguished in them the spirit of faith, and
tormented them with the flames of the nethermost fire.
And this for no other reason except that Israel refused to
apprehend the meaning of such words as have been

revealed in the Bible concerning the signs of the coming Revelation. As she never grasped their true significance, and, to outward seeming, such events never came to pass, she, therefore, remained deprived of recognizing the beauty of Jesus and of beholding the Face of God. And they still await His coming! From time immemorial even unto this day, all the kindreds and peoples of the earth have clung to such fanciful and unseemly thoughts, and thus have deprived themselves of the clear waters streaming from the springs of purity and holiness . . . [17]

To them that are endowed with understanding, it is clear and manifest that, when the fire of the love of Jesus consumed the veils of Jewish limitations, and His authority was made apparent and partially enforced, He, the Revealer of the unseen Beauty, addressing one day His disciples, referred unto His passing, and, kindling in their hearts the fire of bereavement, said unto them: 'I go away and come again unto you.' And in another place He said: 'I go and another will come, Who will tell you all that I have not told you, and will fulfil all that I have said.' Both these sayings have but one meaning, were ye to ponder upon the Manifestations of the Unity of God with Divine insight.

Every discerning observer will recognize that in the Dispensation of the Qur'án both the Book and the Cause of Jesus were confirmed. As to the matter of names, Muḥammad, Himself, declared: 'I am Jesus.' He recognized the truth of the signs, prophecies, and words of Jesus, and testified that they were all of God. In this sense, neither the person of Jesus nor His writings hath differed from that of Muḥammad and of His holy Book, inasmuch as both have championed the Cause of God, uttered His praise, and revealed His commandments. Thus it is that Jesus, Himself, declared: 'I go away and come again unto you.' Consider the sun. Were it to say now, 'I am the sun of yesterday', it would speak the truth. And should it, bearing the sequence of time in mind, claim to be other than that sun, it still would speak the truth. In like manner, if it be said that all the days are but one and the same, it is correct and true. And if it be said, with respect to their particular names and designations, that they differ, that again is true. For though they are the same, yet one doth recognize in each a separate designation, a specific attribute, a particular character. Conceive accordingly the distinction, variation, and unity characteristic of the various Manifestations of holiness, that thou mayest comprehend the allusions made by the Creator of all names and attributes to the mysteries of distinction and unity, and discover the answer to thy question as to why that everlasting Beauty should have, at sundry times, called Himself by different names and titles . . . [19–20]

When the Unseen, the Eternal, the Divine Essence, caused the Day Star of Muḥammad to rise above the horizon of knowledge, among the cavils which the Jewish divines raised against Him was that after Moses no Prophet should be sent of God. Yea, mention hath been made in the Scriptures of a Soul Who must needs be made manifest and Who will advance the Faith, and promote the interests of the people of Moses, so that the Law of the Mosaic Dispensation may encompass the whole earth. Thus hath the King of eternal glory referred in His Book to the words uttered by those wanderers in the vale of remoteness and error: '"The hand of God", say the Jews, "is chained up." Chained up be their own hands; And for that which they have said, they were accursed. Nay, outstretched are both His hands!' 'The hand of God is above their hands.' Although the commentators of the Qur'án have related in divers manners the circumstances attending the revelation of this verse, yet thou shouldst endeavour to apprehend the purpose thereof. He saith: How false is that which the Jews have imagined! How can the hand of Him Who is the King in truth, Who caused the countenance of Moses to be made manifest, and conferred upon Him the robe of Prophethood – how can the hand of such a One be chained and fettered? How can He be conceived as powerless to raise up yet another Messenger after Moses? Behold the absurdity of their saying; how far it hath strayed from the path of knowledge and understanding! Observe how in this Day also, all these people have occupied themselves with such foolish absurdities. For over a thousand years they have been reciting this verse, and unwittingly pronouncing their censure against the Jews, utterly unaware that they themselves, openly and privily, are voicing the sentiments and belief of the Jewish people! Thou art surely aware of their idle contention, that all Revelation is ended, that the portals of Divine mercy are closed, that from the day springs of eternal holiness no Sun shall rise again, that the Ocean of everlasting bounty is forever stilled, and that out of the Tabernacle of ancient glory the Messengers of God have ceased to be made manifest. Such is the measure of the understanding of these small-minded, contemptible people. These people have imagined that the flow of God's all-encompassing grace and plenteous mercies, the cessation of which no mind can contemplate, has been halted. From every side they have risen and girded up the loins of tyranny, and exerted the utmost endeavour to quench with the bitter waters of their vain fancy the flame of God's Burning Bush, oblivious that the globe of power shall, within its own mighty stronghold, protect the Lamp of God . . . [147–8]

Behold how the sovereignty of Muḥammad, the Messenger of God, is today apparent and manifest amongst the people. You are well aware of what befell His Faith in the early days of His Dispensation. What woeful sufferings did the hand of the infidel and erring, the divines of that age and their associates, inflict upon that spiritual Essence, that most pure and holy Being! How abundant the thorns and briars which they have strewn over His path! It is evident that that wretched generation, in their wicked and satanic fancy, regarded every injury to that immortal Being as a means to the attainment of an abiding felicity; inasmuch as the recognized divines of that age, such as 'Abdu'lláh-i-Ubayy, Abú 'Ámír, the hermit, Ka'b-ibn-i-Ashraf, and Naḍr-ibn-i-Ḥárith, all treated Him as an impostor, and pronounced Him a lunatic and a calumniator. Such sore accusations they brought against Him that in recounting them God forbiddeth the ink to flow, Our pen to move, or the page to bear them. These malicious imputations provoked the people to arise and torment Him. And how fierce that torment, if the divines of the age be its chief instigators, if they denounce Him to their followers, cast Him out from their midst, and declare Him a miscreant! Hath not the same befallen this Servant, and been witnessed by all?

For this reason did Muḥammad cry out: 'No Prophet

of God hath suffered such harm as I have suffered.' And
in the Qur'án are recorded all the calumnies and re-
proaches uttered against Him, as well as all the afflictions
which He suffered. Refer ye thereunto, that haply ye may
be informed of that which hath befallen His Revelation.
So grievous was His plight, that for a time all ceased to
hold intercourse with Him and His companions. Whoever
associated with Him fell a victim to the relentless cruelty
of His enemies . . . [114–15]

Consider, how great is the change today! Behold, how
many are the Sovereigns who bow the knee before His
name! How numerous the nations and kingdoms who have
sought the shelter of His shadow, who bear allegiance to
His Faith, and pride themselves therein! From the pulpit-
top there ascendeth today the words of praise which, in
utter lowliness, glorify His blessed name; and from the
heights of minarets there resoundeth the call that
summoneth the concourse of His people to adore Him.
Even those Kings of the earth who have refused to em-
brace His Faith and to put off the garment of unbelief,
none-the-less confess and acknowledge the greatness and
overpowering majesty of that Day Star of loving-kindness.
Such is His earthly sovereignty, the evidences of which
thou dost on every side behold. This sovereignty must
needs be revealed and established either in the lifetime
of every Manifestation of God or after His ascension unto
His true habitation in the realms above . . . [117]

It is evident that the changes brought about in every
Dispensation constitute the dark clouds that intervene
between the eye of man's understanding and the Divine
Luminary which shineth forth from the day spring of the
Divine Essence. Consider how men for generations have
been blindly imitating their fathers, and have been trained
according to such ways and manners as have been laid
down by the dictates of their Faith. Were these men,
therefore, to discover suddenly that a Man, Who hath been
living in their midst, Who, with respect to every human
limitation hath been their equal, had risen to abolish every
established principle imposed by their Faith – principles
by which for centuries they have been disciplined, and
every opposer and denier of which they have come to
regard as infidel, profligate and wicked, – they would of

a certainty be veiled and hindered from acknowledging His truth. Such things are as 'clouds' that veil the eyes of those whose inner being hath not tasted the Salsabíl of detachment, nor drunk from the Kawthar of the knowledge of God. Such men, when acquainted with those circumstances, become so veiled that, without the least question, they pronounce the Manifestation of God as infidel, and sentence Him to death. You must have heard of such things taking place all down the ages, and are now observing them in these days.

It behoveth us, therefore, to make the utmost endeavour, that, by God's invisible assistance, these dark veils, these clouds of Heaven-sent trials, may not hinder us from beholding the beauty of His shining Countenance, and that we may recognize Him only by His own Self. [81–2][54]

Gleanings, Section XIX, pp. 46–9

To every discerning and illuminated heart it is evident that God, the unknowable Essence, the Divine Being, is immensely exalted beyond every human attribute, such as corporeal existence, ascent and descent, egress and regress. Far be it from His glory that human tongue should adequately recount His praise, or that human heart comprehend His fathomless mystery. He is, and hath ever been, veiled in the ancient eternity of His Essence, and will remain in His Reality everlastingly hidden from the sight of men. 'No vision taketh in Him, but He taketh in all vision; He is the Subtile, the All-Perceiving.' . . . [104]

The door of the knowledge of the Ancient of Days being thus closed in the face of all beings, the Source of infinite grace, according to His saying, 'His grace hath transcended all things; My grace hath encompassed them all', hath caused those luminous Gems of Holiness to appear out of the realm of the spirit, in the noble form of the human temple, and be made manifest unto all men, that they may impart unto the world the mysteries of the unchangeable Being, and tell of the subtleties of His imperishable Essence.

These sanctified Mirrors, these Day Springs of ancient

glory, are, one and all, the Exponents on earth of Him
Who is the central Orb of the universe, its Essence and
ultimate Purpose. From Him proceed their knowledge and
power; from Him is derived their sovereignty. The beauty
of their countenance is but a reflection of His image, and
their revelation a sign of His deathless glory. They are the
Treasuries of Divine knowledge, and the Repositories of
celestial wisdom. Through them is transmitted a grace that
is infinite, and by them is revealed the Light that can never
fade . . . [106] These Tabernacles of Holiness, these Primal
Mirrors which reflect the light of unfading glory, are but
expressions of Him Who is the Invisible of the Invisibles.
By the revelation of these Gems of Divine virtue all the
names and attributes of God, such as knowledge and
power, sovereignty and dominion, mercy and wisdom,
glory, bounty, and grace, are made manifest.

    These attributes of God are not, and have never been,
vouchsafed specially unto certain Prophets, and withheld
from others. Nay, all the Prophets of God, His well-favoured, His holy and chosen Messengers are, without
exception, the bearers of His names, and the embodiments
of His attributes. They only differ in the intensity of their
revelation, and the comparative potency of their light.
Even as He hath revealed: 'Some of the Apostles We have
caused to excel the others.'

    It hath, therefore, become manifest and evident that
within the tabernacles of these Prophets and chosen Ones
of God the light of His infinite names and exalted attributes hath been reflected, even though the light of some of
these attributes may or may not be outwardly revealed
from these luminous Temples to the eyes of men. That a
certain attribute of God hath not been outwardly manifested by these Essences of Detachment doth in no wise
imply that they who are the Day Springs of God's attributes and the Treasuries of His holy names did not actually
possess it. Therefore, these illuminated Souls, these beauteous Countenances have, each and every one of them,
been endowed with all the attributes of God, such as
sovereignty, dominion, and the like, even though to
outward seeming they be shorn of all earthly majesty . . .
[109–11][55]

Gleanings, Section XXII, pp. 50–6

The Bearers of the Trust of God are made manifest unto the peoples of the earth as the Exponents of a new Cause and the Revealers of a new Message. Inasmuch as these Birds of the celestial Throne are all sent down from the heaven of the Will of God, and as they all arise to proclaim His irresistible Faith, they, therefore, are regarded as one soul and the same person. For they all drink from the one Cup of the love of God, and all partake of the fruit of the same Tree of Oneness.

These Manifestations of God have each a twofold station. One is the station of pure abstraction and essential unity. In this respect, if thou callest them all by one name, and dost ascribe to them the same attributes, thou hast not erred from the truth. Even as He hath revealed: 'No distinction do We make between any of His Messengers.' For they, one and all, summon the people of the earth to acknowledge the unity of God, and herald unto them the Kawthar of an infinite grace and bounty. They are all invested with the robe of prophethood, and are honoured with the mantle of glory. Thus hath Muḥammad, the Point of the Qur'án, revealed: 'I am all the Prophets.' Likewise, He saith: 'I am the first Adam, Noah, Moses, and Jesus.' Similar statements have been made by Imám 'Alí. Sayings such as these, which indicate the essential unity of those Exponents of Oneness, have also emanated from the Channels of God's immortal utterance, and the Treasuries of the gems of Divine knowledge, and have been recorded in the Scriptures. These Countenances are the recipients of the Divine Command, and the Day Springs of His Revelation. This Revelation is exalted above the veils of plurality and the exigencies of number. Thus He saith: 'Our Cause is but One.' Inasmuch as the Cause is one and the same, the Exponents thereof also must needs be one and the same. Likewise, the Imáms of the Muḥammadan Faith, those lamps of certitude, have said: 'Muḥammad is our first, Muḥammad is our last, Muḥammad our all.'

It is clear and evident to thee that all the Prophets are the Temples of the Cause of God, Who have appeared clothed in divers attire. If thou wilt observe with discriminating eyes, thou wilt behold Them all abiding in the same tabernacle, soaring in the same heaven, seated upon the same throne, uttering the same speech, and proclaiming the same Faith. Such is the unity of those Essences of Being, those Luminaries of infinite and immeasurable splendour! Wherefore, should one of these Manifestations of Holiness proclaim saying: 'I am the return of all the Prophets', He, verily, speaketh the truth. In like manner, in every subsequent Revelation, the return of the former Revelation is a fact, the truth of which is firmly established . . . [161–2]

The other station is the station of distinction, and pertaineth to the world of creation, and to the limitations thereof. In this respect, each Manifestation of God hath a distinct individuality, a definitely prescribed mission, a predestined revelation, and specially designated limitations. Each one of them is known by a different name, is characterized by a special attribute, fulfils a definite mission, and is entrusted with a particular Revelation. Even as He saith: 'Some of the Apostles We have caused to excel the others. To some God hath spoken, some He hath raised and exalted. And to Jesus, Son of Mary, We gave manifest signs, and We strengthened Him with the Holy Spirit.'

It is because of this difference in their station and mission that the words and utterances flowing from these Well Springs of Divine knowledge appear to diverge and differ. Otherwise, in the eyes of them that are initiated into the mysteries of Divine wisdom, all their utterances are, in reality, but the expressions of one Truth. As most of the people have failed to appreciate those stations to which We have referred, they, therefore, feel perplexed and dismayed at the varying utterances pronounced by Manifestations that are essentially one and the same.

It hath ever been evident that all these divergencies of utterance are attributable to differences of station. Thus, viewed from the standpoint of their oneness and sublime detachment, the attributes of Godhead, Divinity, Supreme Singleness, and Inmost Essence, have been, and are applicable to those Essences of Being, inasmuch as they all abide on the throne of Divine Revelation, and are established upon the seat of Divine Concealment. Through their appearance the Revelation of God is made manifest, and by their countenance the Beauty of God is revealed. Thus it is that the accents of God Himself have been heard uttered by these Manifestations of the Divine Being.

Viewed in the light of their second station – the station of distinction, differentiation, temporal limitations, characteristics and standards – they manifest absolute servitude, utter destitution, and complete self-effacement. Even as He saith: 'I am the servant of God. I am but a man like you.' . . . [191–4]

Were any of the all-embracing Manifestations of God to declare: 'I am God', He, verily, speaketh the truth, and no doubt attacheth thereto. For it hath been repeatedly demonstrated that through their Revelation, their attributes and names, the Revelation of God, His names and His attributes, are made manifest in the world. Thus, He hath revealed: 'Those shafts were God's, not Thine.' And also He saith: 'In truth, they who plighted fealty unto Thee, really plighted that fealty unto God.' And were any of them to voice the utterance, 'I am the Messenger of God', He, also, speaketh the truth, the indubitable truth. Even as He saith: 'Muḥammad is not the father of any man among you, but He is the Messenger of God.' Viewed in this light, they are all but Messengers of that ideal King, that unchangeable Essence. And were they all to proclaim, 'I am the Seal of the Prophets', they, verily, utter but the truth, beyond the faintest shadow of doubt. For they are all but one person, one soul, one spirit, one being, one revelation. They are all the manifestation of the 'Beginning' and the 'End', the 'First' and the 'Last', the 'Seen' and the 'Hidden' – all of which pertain to Him Who is the Innermost Spirit of Spirits and Eternal Essence of Essences. And were they to say, 'We are the Servants of God', this also is a manifest and indisputable fact. For they have been made manifest in the uttermost state of servitude, a servitude the like of which no man can possibly attain. Thus in moments in which these Essences of Being were deep immersed beneath the oceans of ancient and everlasting holiness, or when they soared to the loftiest summits of Divine mysteries, they claimed their utterances to be the Voice of Divinity, the Call of God Himself.

Were the eye of discernment to be opened, it would

recognize that in this very state, they have considered
themselves utterly effaced and non-existent in the face of
Him Who is the All-Pervading, the Incorruptible. Methinks, they have regarded themselves as utter nothingness, and deemed their mention in that Court an act of
blasphemy. For the slightest whispering of self within such
a Court is an evidence of self-assertion and independent
existence. In the eyes of them that have attained unto that
Court, such a suggestion is itself a grievous transgression.
How much more grievous would it be, were aught else to
be mentioned in that Presence, were man's heart, his
tongue, his mind, or his soul, to be busied with any one but
the Well-Beloved, were his eyes to behold any countenance
other than His beauty, were his ear to be inclined to any
melody but His Voice, and were his feet to tread any way
but His way . . . [196]

By virtue of this station they have claimed for themselves the Voice of Divinity and the like, whilst by virtue
of their station of Messengership, they have declared
themselves the Messengers of God. In every instance they
have voiced an utterance that would conform to the requirements of the occasion, and have ascribed all these
declarations to Themselves, declarations ranging from the
realm of Divine Revelation to the realm of creation, and
from the domain of Divinity even unto the domain of
earthly existence. Thus it is that whatsoever be their
utterance, whether it pertain to the realm of Divinity,
Lordship, Prophethood, Messengership, Guardianship,
Apostleship, or Servitude, all is true, beyond the shadow
of a doubt. Therefore these sayings which We have quoted
in support of Our argument must be attentively considered, that the divergent utterances of the Manifestations
of the Unseen and Day Springs of Holiness may cease to
agitate the soul and perplex the mind. [198][56]

Gleanings, Section XC, pp. 177–9

Whatever is in the heavens and whatever is on the earth
is a direct evidence of the revelation within it of the attributes and names of God, inasmuch as within every atom
are enshrined the signs that bear eloquent testimony to the

revelation of that Most Great Light. Methinks, but for the potency of that revelation, no being could ever exist. How resplendent the luminaries of knowledge that shine in an atom, and how vast the oceans of wisdom that surge within a drop! To a supreme degree is this true of man, who, among all created things, hath been invested with the robe of such gifts, and hath been singled out for the glory of such distinction. For in him are potentially revealed all the attributes and names of God to a degree that no other created being hath excelled or surpassed. All these names and attributes are applicable to him. Even as He hath said: 'Man is My mystery, and I am his mystery.' Manifold are the verses that have been repeatedly revealed in all the Heavenly Books and the Holy Scriptures, expressive of this most subtle and lofty theme. Even as He hath revealed: 'We will surely show them Our signs in the world and within themselves.' Again He saith: 'And also in your own selves: will ye not, then, behold the signs of God?' And yet again He revealeth: 'And be ye not like those who forget God, and whom He hath therefore caused to forget their own selves.' In this connection, He Who is the eternal King – may the souls of all that dwell within the mystic Tabernacle be a sacrifice unto Him – hath spoken: 'He hath known God who hath known himself.' [107]

. . . From that which hath been said it becometh evident that all things, in their inmost reality, testify to the revelation of the names and attributes of God within them. Each according to its capacity, indicateth, and is expressive of, the knowledge of God. So potent and universal is this revelation, that it hath encompassed all things visible and invisible. Thus hath He revealed: 'Hath aught else save Thee a power of revelation which is not possessed by Thee, that it could have manifested Thee? Blind is the eye which doth not perceive Thee.' Likewise hath the eternal King spoken: 'No thing have I perceived, except that I perceived God within it, God before it, or God after it.' Also in the tradition of Kumayl it is written: 'Behold, a light hath shone forth out of the morn of eternity, and lo, its waves have penetrated the inmost reality of all men.' Man, the noblest and most perfect of all created things, excelleth them all in the intensity of this revelation, and is a fuller expression of its glory. And of all men, the most accomplished, the most distinguished, and the most excellent are the Manifestations of the Sun of Truth. Nay, all else besides these Manifestations, live by the operation of Their Will, and move and have their being through the outpourings of Their grace. [109][57]

Gleanings, Section XCI, pp. 179–83

Amongst the proofs demonstrating the truth of this Revelation is this, that in every age and Dispensation, whenever the invisible Essence was revealed in the person of His Manifestation, certain souls, obscure and detached from all worldly entanglements, would seek illumination from the Sun of Prophethood and Moon of Divine guidance, and would attain unto the Divine Presence. For this reason, the divines of the age and those possessed of wealth, would scorn and scoff at these people. Even as He hath revealed concerning them that erred: 'Then said the chiefs of His people who believed not, "We see in Thee but a man like ourselves; and we see not any who have followed Thee except our meanest ones of hasty judgement, nor see we any excellence in you above ourselves: nay, we deem you liars."' They cavilled at those holy Manifestations, and protested saying: 'None hath followed you except the abject amongst us, those who are worthy of no attention.' Their aim was to show that no one amongst the learned, the wealthy, and the renowned believed in them. By this and similar proofs they sought to demonstrate the falsity of Him that speaketh naught but the truth.

In this most resplendent Dispensation, however, this most mighty Sovereignty, a number of illumined divines, of men of consummate learning, of doctors of mature wisdom, have attained unto His Court, drunk the cup of His divine Presence, and been invested with the honour of His most excellent favour. They have renounced, for the sake of the Beloved, the world and all that is therein . . . [246–7]

All these were guided by the light of the Sun of Divine Revelation, confessed and acknowledged His truth. Such was their faith, that most of them renounced their substance and kindred, and cleaved to the good pleasure of the All-Glorious. They laid down their lives for their Well-Beloved, and surrendered their all in His path. Their breasts were made targets for the darts of the enemy, and their heads adorned the spears of the infidel. No land remained which did not drink the blood of these embodiments of detachment, and no sword that did not bruise their necks. Their deeds, alone, testify to the truth of their words. Doth not the testimony of these holy souls, who have so gloriously risen to offer up their lives for their Beloved that the whole world marvelled at the manner of their sacrifice, suffice the people of this day? Is it not sufficient witness against the faithlessness of those who for a trifle betrayed their faith, who bartered away immortality for that which perisheth, who gave up the Kawthar of the Divine Presence for salty springs, and whose one aim in life is to usurp the property of others? Even as thou dost witness how all of them have busied themselves with the vanities of the world, and have strayed far from Him Who is the Lord, the Most High.

Be fair: Is the testimony of those acceptable and worthy of attention whose deeds agree with their words, whose outward behaviour conforms with their inner life? The mind is bewildered at their deeds, and the soul marvelleth at their fortitude and bodily endurance. Or is the testimony of these faithless souls who breathe naught but the breath of selfish desire, and who lie imprisoned in the cage of their idle fancies, acceptable? Like the bats of darkness, they lift not their heads from their couch except to pursue the transient things of the world, and find no rest by night except as they labour to advance the aims of their sordid life. Immersed in their selfish schemes, they are oblivious of the Divine decree. In the daytime they strive with all their soul after worldly benefits, and in the night season their sole occupation is to gratify their carnal desires. By what law or standard could men be justified in cleaving to the denials of such petty-minded souls and in ignoring the faith of them that have renounced, for the sake of the good pleasure of God, their life and substance, their fame and renown, their reputation and honour? . . . [249–50]

With what love, what devotion, what exultation and holy rapture, they sacrificed their lives in the path of the All-Glorious! To the truth of this all witness. And yet, how can they belittle this Revelation? Hath any age witnessed such momentous happenings? If these companions be not the true strivers after God, who else could be called by this name? Have these companions been seekers after power or glory? Have they ever yearned for riches? Have they cherished any desire except the good pleasure of God? If these companions, with all their marvellous testimonies and wondrous works, be false, who then is worthy to claim for himself the truth? I swear by God! Their very deeds are a sufficient testimony, and an irrefutable proof unto all the peoples of the earth, were men to ponder in their hearts the mysteries of Divine Revelation. 'And they who act unjustly shall soon know what lot awaiteth them!' . . . [251]

Consider these martyrs of unquestionable sincerity, to whose truthfulness testifieth the explicit text of the Book, and all of whom, as thou hast witnessed, have sacrificed their life, their substance, their wives, their children, their all, and ascended unto the loftiest chambers of Paradise. Is it fair to reject the testimony of these detached and exalted beings to the truth of this pre-eminent and Glorious Revelation, and to regard as acceptable the denunciations which have been uttered against this resplendent Light by this faithless people, who for gold have forsaken their faith, and who for the sake of leadership have repudiated Him Who is the First Leader of all mankind? This, although their character is now revealed unto all people who have recognized them as those who will in no wise relinquish one jot or one tittle of their temporal authority for the sake of God's holy Faith, how much less their life, their substance, and the like. [252][58]

Gleanings, Section CXXV, pp. 264–70

O My brother! When a true seeker determineth to take the step of search in the path leading unto the knowledge of the Ancient of Days, he must, before all else, cleanse his heart, which is the seat of the revelation of the inner mysteries of God, from the obscuring dust of all acquired knowledge, and the allusions of the embodiments of satanic fancy. He must purge his breast, which is the sanctuary of the abiding love of the Beloved, of every

defilement, and sanctify his soul from all that pertaineth
to water and clay, from all shadowy and ephemeral attachments. He must so cleanse his heart that no remnant of
either love or hate may linger therein, lest that love blindly
incline him to error, or that hate repel him away from the
truth. Even as thou dost witness in this Day how most of
the people, because of such love and hate, are bereft of the
immortal Face, have strayed far from the Embodiments
of the Divine mysteries, and, shepherdless, are roaming
through the wilderness of oblivion and error.

That seeker must, at all times, put his trust in God,
must renounce the peoples of the earth, must detach
himself from the world of dust, and cleave unto Him Who
is the Lord of Lords. He must never seek to exalt himself
above any one, must wash away from the tablet of his heart
every trace of pride and vain-glory, must cling unto pa-
tience and resignation, observe silence and refrain from
idle talk. For the tongue is a smouldering fire, and excess
of speech a deadly poison. Material fire consumeth the
body, whereas the fire of the tongue devoureth both heart
and soul. The force of the former lasteth but for a time,
whilst the effects of the latter endureth a century.

That seeker should, also, regard backbiting as grievous
error, and keep himself aloof from its dominion, inasmuch
as backbiting quencheth the light of the heart, and
extinguisheth the life of the soul. He should be content
with little, and be freed from all inordinate desire. He
should treasure the companionship of them that have
renounced the world, and regard avoidance of boastful
and worldly people a precious benefit. At the dawn of
every day he should commune with God, and, with all his
soul, persevere in the quest of his Beloved. He should
consume every wayward thought with the flame of His
loving mention, and, with the swiftness of lightning, pass
by all else save Him. He should succour the dispossessed,
and never withhold his favour from the destitute. He
should show kindness to animals, how much more unto his
fellow-man, to him who is endowed with the power of
utterance. He should not hesitate to offer up his life for his
Beloved, nor allow the censure of the people to turn him
away from the Truth. He should not wish for others that
which he doth not wish for himself, nor promise that which

he doth not fulfil. With all his heart he should avoid fellowship with evil-doers, and pray for the remission of their sins. He should forgive the sinful, and never despise his low estate, for none knoweth what his own end shall be. How often hath a sinner attained, at the hour of death, to the essence of faith, and, quaffing the immortal draught, hath taken his flight unto the Concourse on high! And how often hath a devout believer, at the hour of his soul's ascension, been so changed as to fall into the nethermost fire!

Our purpose in revealing these convincing and weighty utterances is to impress upon the seeker that he should regard all else beside God as transient, and count all things save Him, Who is the Object of all adoration, as utter nothingness.

These are among the attributes of the exalted, and constitute the hall-mark of the spiritually-minded. They have already been mentioned in connection with the requirements of the wayfarers that tread the path of Positive Knowledge. When the detached wayfarer and sincere seeker hath fulfilled these essential conditions, then and only then can he be called a true seeker. Whensoever he hath fulfilled the conditions implied in the verse: 'Whoso maketh efforts for Us', he shall enjoy the blessings conferred by the words: 'In Our Ways shall We assuredly guide him.'

Only when the lamp of search, of earnest striving, of longing desire, of passionate devotion, of fervid love, of rapture, and ecstasy, is kindled within the seeker's heart, and the breeze of His loving-kindness is wafted upon his soul, will the darkness of error be dispelled, the mists of doubts and misgivings be dissipated, and the lights of knowledge and certitude envelop his being. At that hour will the Mystic Herald, bearing the joyful tidings of the Spirit, shine forth from the City of God resplendent as the morn, and, through the trumpet-blast of knowledge, will awaken the heart, the soul, and the spirit from the slumber of heedlessness. Then will the manifold favours and outpouring grace of the holy and everlasting Spirit confer such new life upon the seeker that he will find himself endowed with a new eye, a new ear, a new heart, and a new mind. He will contemplate the manifest signs of the universe, and will penetrate the hidden mysteries of the soul. Gazing with the eye of God, he will perceive within every atom a door that leadeth him to the stations of absolute certitude. He will discover in all things the mysteries of Divine Revelation, and the evidences of an everlasting Manifestation.

I swear by God! Were he that treadeth the path of guidance and seeketh to scale the heights of righteousness to attain unto this glorious and exalted station, he would inhale, at a distance of a thousand leagues, the fragrance of God, and would perceive the resplendent morn of a divine Guidance rising above the dayspring of all things. Each and every thing, however small, would be to him a revelation, leading him to his Beloved, the Object of his quest. So great shall be the discernment of this seeker that he will discriminate between truth and falsehood, even as he doth distinguish the sun from shadow. If in the uttermost corners of the East the sweet savours of God be wafted, he will assuredly recognize and inhale their fragrance, even though he be dwelling in the uttermost ends of the West. He will, likewise, clearly distinguish all the signs of God – His wondrous utterances, His great works, and mighty deeds – from the doings, the words and ways of men, even as the jeweller who knoweth the gem from the stone, or the man who distinguisheth the spring from autumn, and heat from cold. When the channel of the human soul is cleansed of all worldly and impeding attachments, it will unfailingly perceive the breath of the Beloved across immeasurable distances, and will, led by its perfume, attain and enter the City of Certitude.

Therein he will discern the wonders of His ancient Wisdom, and will perceive all the hidden teachings from the rustling leaves of the Tree that flourisheth in that City. With both his inner and outer ear, he will hear from its dust the hymns of glory and praise ascending unto the Lord of Lords, and with his inner eye will he discover the mysteries of 'return' and 'revival'.

How unspeakably glorious are the signs, the tokens, the revelations, and splendours which He, Who is the King of Names and Attributes, hath destined for that City! The attainment unto this City quencheth thirst without water, and kindleth the love of God without fire. Within every blade of grass are enshrined the mysteries of an inscrutable Wisdom, and upon every rose-bush a myriad nightingales pour out, in blissful rapture, their melody. Its wondrous tulips unfold the mystery of the undying Fire in the Burning Bush, and its sweet savours of holiness breathe the perfume of the Messianic Spirit. It bestoweth wealth without gold, and conferreth immortality without death. In each one of its leaves ineffable delights are treasured, and within every chamber unnumbered mysteries lie hidden.

They that valiantly labour in quest of God, will, when once they have renounced all else but Him, be so attached and wedded unto that City, that a moment's separation from it would to them be unthinkable. They will hearken unto infallible proofs from the Hyacinth of that assembly, and will receive the surest testimonies from the beauty of its Rose, and the melody of its Nightingale. Once in about a thousand years shall this City be renewed and readorned . . . [213–18]

That City is none other than the Word of God revealed in every age and dispensation. In the days of Moses it was the Pentateuch; in the days of Jesus, the Gospel; in the days of Muḥammad, the Messenger of God, the Qur'án; in this day, the Bayán; and in the Dispensation of Him Whom God will make manifest, His own Book – the Book unto which all the Books of former Dispensations must needs be referred, the Book that standeth amongst them all transcendent and supreme. [210][59]

4

A Sequential Outline of the Text

The following outline represents one effort to identify the important subject matter of the Íqán in the order in which it appears in the text. The task is formidable. The outline is not intended to be fully comprehensive but, rather, to serve as an aid to locating various subjects. It is suggested the student should consider preparing his own version. It proves a very helpful exercise in coming to an understanding of the structure of the book as a whole and leads to an appreciation of how the Íqán is composed of a number of themes, all intricately interwoven. This sequential approach does not deal adequately with this interweaving. Section 3 of this study offers references indicating the flow of some of these themes and section 5 provides a topical outline. The items below are accompanied by paragraph numbers from the Íqán.

Part One

Detachment is the key to true understanding   1, 2

Requirements of those who tread the path of faith   2

Words and deeds of men are no standard for understanding and recognition of God and His Prophets   2

Cause of denial of Prophets of the past   3–6

    Súrih of Húd surely sufficeth   5

5

A Topical Approach to the Study of the Íqán

Some years ago the Hand of the Cause Horace Holley prepared a study guide to the Íqán grouping various points under five separate topics. This approach provides an important alternative to the sequential arrangement found in section 4. Essentially, it presents the major themes set out by Shoghi Effendi (see section 3) under different headings and with more detail. The outline is reproduced here in full as found in the guide except that paragraphs numbers have been substituted for the original page numbers.

I. The Path of Faith (Paragraphs 1–18; 213–19)

They that tread the path of faith 2
Consider the past 3–6
The indignities heaped upon the Prophets of God 6
    Noah 7–8, Húd 9, Ṣáliḥ 10, Abraham 11, Moses 12, Jesus 17, 19
Advent of every true Manifestation accompanied by strife 13
Whatever in days gone by hath been the cause of denial 14
Leaders of religion have hindered their people 16
The true meaning is revealed to none except those that manifest 16
Thus hath God laid hold of them for their sins 17
The attributes of the exalted 215

III. God in Manifestation (Paragraphs 103–28; 131–47;
191–212; 256–80)

The Luminaries of truth are endowed with an all-compel-
    ling power 103

They that have hearts to understand 280

IV. The Presence of God (Paragraphs 148–56; 181–90)

How can He be conceived as powerless? 149

The essential Purpose and the knowledge of the Mystery
    and Substance of the Cause of God . . . attaining unto
    the Presence of God 148, Day of Resurrection 149,
    Most Holy Outpouring 150, Holy Outpouring 151,
    Attaining to the presence of these Holy Luminaries
    151, No day is mightier than this Day 153, How can
    he be called learned? 154, Sign of the Day of Revela-
    tion 155, Testimony of the Qur'án 181, Resurrection
    and attainment unto His Presence 182, Respite to an
    appointed time 182–4, 1280 years have passed 185,
    How the peoples are brought to a reckoning 186–7

Able to unfold innumerable mysteries 190

V. The Return (Paragraphs 128–30; 156–79)

The purpose of the Prophets to affirm the spiritual signifi-
    cance of the terms 'life', 'resurrection' and 'judge-
    ment' 128

Only those will attain the knowledge of the Word of God
    that have turned unto Him 130

Unnumbered doors of knowledge set open 156

Already have Apostles before me come to you 157

    How could those people in the days of Muḥammad
    have existed thousands of years before? 157–9, If
    Muḥammad was the 'return' of the Prophets, His
    Companions must be the 'return' of the bygone
    Companions 160, The Prophets regarded as one soul
    and the same person 161–2, The return of their
    chosen ones definitely proved 162, The people so
    transformed that they renounce all things 163, Have
    not this people exemplified the mysteries of 'rebirth'

6

Annotations to the Íqán

The following annotations should in no wise be considered as conclusive or comprehensive. Obviously no one is in a position to compose an authoritative commentary on the revealed Books of God. Rather, these notes, related as they are in one way or another to points and themes in the text of the Íqán, are intended to help stimulate the reader in considering the various truths set forth and encourage the student to seek out from the vast ocean of the Bahá'í writings such verses and passages as will throw further light on the subjects at hand.

Several verses quoted by Bahá'u'lláh in the Íqán are not identified in the text. Most of these are from the reported sayings or ḥadíth of the Prophet Muḥammad and His legitimate successors, the twelve Imáms. Of those attributed to Muḥammad there are two classifications: those that are said to be from Himself, and those that are the Voice of God. The latter are known as Ḥadíth-i-Qudsí (Holy Traditions) and are so indicated in the annotations. As will be seen, some of the material cited is from Bahá'u'lláh Himself and is set off by quotation marks either because it is a quote from elsewhere or it is a passage in Arabic. The identifications provided are, for the most part, on the authority of Ishráq Khávarí's four-volume encyclopedic Persian study, the *Qámús-i-Íqán*.

The numbers in the left hand column refer to paragraphs of the Íqán.

Part One

The Book of Certitude is divided into two parts. Each is headed by a brief paragraph which sets out its general theme. Part One centres on the importance of detachment in attaining to true understanding of God and His Prophets; an account of the cruelties suffered by the divine Messengers; the consequences of people blindly following religious leaders and not searching out truth for themselves; the exalted station of the Manifestations of God; the method of God in trying His servants to distinguish the sincere from the false; and the relativity of religious truth, as well as the continuity of divine Revelation.

> Invocation **the Exalted, the Most High** (Arabic: 'Alíyyu'l-A'lá) Names of God often associated with the Báb Himself as in the 'battle cry' animating the heroes and heroines of the Ten Year Spiritual Crusade (1953–63): 'Yá-Bahá'u'l-Abhá, Yá Alíyyu'l-A'lá.'[60]

> 1 **No man shall attain** This opening paragraph, like the one that heads Part Two of the Íqán, was revealed by Bahá'u'lláh in Arabic. Both are followed by extensive elucidations in Persian.

> 1 **true understanding** Man's attainment of this understanding is one of the essential animating purposes of creation. Such divine knowledge, such comprehension, wisdom and recognition, as emphasized in the Íqán, is not dependent upon acquired human learning. Rather, true understanding is in the nature of light from the sun of divine knowledge which, shining from the Prophets of God, is reflected in the heart of man, endowing it with the recognition of truth and inspiring it with the comprehension of spiritual realities. As it is said: 'Knowledge is a light which God casteth into the heart of whomsoever

He willeth.'[61] Note the spiritual prerequisites, in this case, detachment and sanctity of soul, which are necessary for a true comprehension of Divine Revelation. The requirement of virtue in connection with the attainment of knowledge and insight is a recurring truth of the Íqán. It is clear that people differ in regard to the degree of true understanding which they have attained. 'Abdu'l-Bahá in a Tablet comments on the relative character of this understanding and establishes that no matter how high the soaring ones fly in the utmost degrees of knowledge and comprehension, no matter how near the worshippers of the one true God ascend towards the summits of certitude, they are but reading letters from the book of their own selves, reaching only to the brilliant unseen signs that are enshrined in the reality of their own beings, and circling round the centre of their own entities. He further emphasizes that the degrees which are beyond their realms of understanding shall never be perceived nor understood by them.[62]

1 **detached from all that is in heaven and on earth**
Desire for either earthly rewards or heavenly treasures constitutes an improper motive for seeking God's good-pleasure. '. . . if thy gaze should be on paradise, and thou shouldst worship Him while cherishing such a hope, thou wouldst make God's creation a partner with Him, notwithstanding the fact that paradise is desired by men.'[63]

1 **Bayán** Literally, 'utterance', 'explanation'. Term used in reference to the whole of the Báb's Revelation as stated in the Persian Bayán: 'The substance of this chapter is this, that all the writings of the Point [i.e. the Báb] are named Beyán.'[64] Bahá'u'lláh Himself

confirms this in the following passage addressed to the Báb:

> Should any one consider Thy Books which Thou didst name the Bayán, and ponder in his heart what hath been revealed therein, he would discover that each of these Books announceth my Revelation, and declareth my Name, and testifieth to my Self, and proclaimeth my Cause, and my Praise, and my Rising, and the radiance of my Glory.[65]

Also the specific title of two important works of the Báb: the above-mentioned Persian Bayán and the Arabic Bayán. See note on the **Persian Bayán** at 219 below.

2 **they that tread the path of faith** Such wayfarers in the path of faith are defined in Islamic mysticism as those who have freed themselves from vain imaginations, have subdued the animal side of their nature, have set foot on the way of faith, and by the aid of God, after passing the seven valleys or cities, as explained by Bahá'u'lláh in the *Seven Valleys*, attain the object of their quest.

2 **certitude** The human soul's realization of certitude is an important theme found not only in the Íqán but throughout Bahá'u'lláh's writings. For example: 'Blessed are they who, on the wings of certitude, have flown in the heavens which the Pen of thy Lord, the All-Merciful, hath spread.'[66] 'He it is Who hath unveiled to your eyes the treasures of His knowledge, and caused you to ascend unto the heaven of certitude – the certitude of His resistless, His irrefutable, and most exalted Faith.'[67] It was He Himself Who chose to identify His principal doctrinal work with the theme of certitude.

2 **a standard** The principle of reference to the revealed Word of God as the balance in determining the truth of things is most powerfully stated by Bahá'u'lláh in His Most Holy Book:

> Weigh not the Book of God with such standards and sciences as are current amongst you, for the Book itself is the unerring Balance established amongst men. In this most perfect Balance whatsoever the peoples and kindreds of the earth possess must be weighed, while the measure of its weight should be tested according to its own standard, did ye but know it.[68]

3 **Manifestations of God** Bahá'í term meaning the Messengers of God, such as Moses, Jesus, Muḥammad, the Báb and Bahá'u'lláh.

> . . . in the kingdoms of earth and heaven there must needs be manifested a Being, an Essence Who shall act as a Manifestation and Vehicle for the transmission of the grace of the Divinity Itself, the Sovereign Lord of all. Through the Teachings of this Day Star of Truth every man will advance and develop until he attaineth the station at which he can manifest all the potential forces with which his inmost true self hath been endowed.[69]

> The Person of the Manifestation hath ever been the representative and mouthpiece of God. He, in truth, is the Day Spring of God's most excellent Titles, and the Dawning-Place of His exalted Attributes.[70]

3 **the face of God** With regard to His own Revelation Bahá'u'lláh proclaims: 'This is the Day whereon naught can be seen except the splendours of the Light that shineth from the face of Thy Lord, the Gracious, the Most Bountiful.'[71] 'He Who, from everlasting, had concealed His Face from the sight of creation is now

come.'[72] 'O ye leaders of religion! Who is the man amongst you that can rival Me in vision or insight? Where is he to be found that dareth to claim to be My equal in utterance or wisdom? No, by My Lord, the All-Merciful! All on the earth shall pass away; and this is the face of your Lord, the Almighty, the Well-Beloved.'[73]

4 **'No Messenger . . . laugh Him to scorn.'** Reference is also made to the scorning of Prophets in the Bible: 'And he said, Verily I say unto you, No prophet is accepted in his own country.'[74] 'A prophet is not without honour, save in his own country, and in his own house.'[75]

5 **possessed of true understanding** See note on the same subject at 1 above.

5 **Súrih of Húd** The eleventh chapter of the Qur'án, 123 verses in length, which recounts the successive calls of God's Prophets and Messengers and the dire consequences befalling those peoples who rejected them. See note on **Húd** at 9 below.

5 **negation** Bahá'u'lláh confirms in one of His meditations with reference to humankind that 'the letters of negation, no matter how far they may be removed from the holy fragrances of Thy knowledge, and however forgetful they may become of the wondrous splendours of the dawning light of Thy beauty, which are shed from the heaven of Thy majesty, must needs exist in Thy realm, so that the words which affirm Thee may thereby be exalted'.[76] The words and deeds of the Prophets, as set out in this part of the Íqán, have been the essential factors effecting this distinction between negation and affirmation. Those who conform

to the Book of God, as explained by the Báb, 'will abide in Paradise, under the shadow of His affirmation and reckoned among the most sublime Letters in the presence of God; while whoso deviateth, were it even so much as the tip of a grain of barley, will be consigned to the fire and will be assembled neath the shadow of negation'.[77]

With regard to the operation of this principle in His own Day, Bahá'u'lláh affirms:

> If all who are in heaven and on earth be invested in this day with the powers and attributes destined for the Letters of the Bayán, whose station is ten thousand times more glorious than that of the Letters of the Qur'ánic Dispensation, and if they one and all should, swift as the twinkling of an eye, hesitate to recognize My Revelation, they shall be accounted, in the sight of God, of those that have gone astray, and regarded as 'Letters of Negation.'[78]

5 **bird of the human heart** 'Wings have I bestowed upon thee, that thou mayest fly to the realms of mystic holiness and not the regions of satanic fancy.'[79] The Bahá'í writings are replete with examples likening the soul of man to a bird. If, we are told, a bird is always soaring higher, its progress will be continual, but if it relaxes in its efforts it will necessarily descend to the earth.[80]

5 **bread** Here we have the inner meaning of manna from heaven as found in past scriptures:

> That which is preeminent above all other gifts, is incorruptible in nature, and pertaineth to God Himself, is the gift of Divine Revelation. Every bounty conferred by the Creator upon man, be it material or spiritual, is subservient unto this. It is, in its essence, and will ever so remain, the Bread which cometh

down from Heaven . . . He hath, indeed, partaken of
this highest gift of God who hath recognized His
Manifestation in this Day.[81]

Thank God that thou wert fed from the table which
hath descended from heaven. That food is 'I am the
bread which descended from heaven', recorded in the
Gospel. That is faith, certainty, love and knowledge.[82]

6 indignities heaped upon the Prophets

Thou hast known how grievously the Prophets of
God, His Messengers and Chosen Ones, have been
afflicted. Meditate a while on the motive and reason
which have been responsible for such a persecution.
At no time, in no Dispensation, have the Prophets of
God escaped the blasphemy of their enemies, the
cruelty of their oppressors, the denunciation of the
learned of their age, who appeared in the guise of
uprightness and piety. Day and night they passed
through such agonies as none can ever measure,
except the knowledge of the one true God, exalted
be His glory.[83]

Such hath been the perversity of men and their
transgressions, so grievous have been the trials that
have afflicted the Prophets of God and their chosen
ones, that all mankind deserveth to be tormented and
to perish. God's hidden and most loving providence,
however, hath, through both visible and invisible
agencies, protected and will continue to protect it
from the penalty of its wickedness.[84]

Note from this paragraph of the Íqán that close obser-
vation of the history of the opposition inflicted on the
Prophets will strengthen one's faith.

7 **Noah** Bahá'u'lláh here begins brief accounts of the
ministries of a number of Prophets starting with Noah.

For additional accounts of Noah see Qur'án 4:163, 7:59, 10:71, 11:25, 23:23–30, 26:105–20; also 37:75, 71:1–28, etc. and the biblical story in Genesis 5–9. 'The Ark and the Flood we believe are symbolical.'[85]

7 **nine hundred and fifty years**

> The Guardian advises, that the period of 950 years referred to in the Íqán, as the time Noah exhorted the people – refers to the period of His Ministry. The term year does not refer to a period of time such as our year – it was entirely different; and thus does not extend over any such period as our present term year would imply.[86]

> Approximately six thousand years have elapsed since the appearance of Adam. The ages of the Prophets specified in the Bible were based on a different calculation than the one used at present. The years mentioned in the Bible were different from ours.[87]

The Bible makes no reference to Noah until He is said to be five hundred years old and when He begets three sons; see Genesis 5:32.

7 **such pain and suffering** According to a tradition attributed to the Imám Ṣádiq, Noah was several times so badly beaten by the infidels that His ears would gush with blood and He would for a time lose consciousness. Noah's followers would beg Him to ask God to punish the unbelievers but Noah would instead pray for them.

7 **the divine promise was not fulfilled** The non-fulfilment of a prophetic announcement owing to a change in the divine purpose (Arabic, *badá*) is an accepted theological principle in Islám and is confirmed in the Bahá'í writings.

With regard to the specific promise mentioned here and recorded in 'the best-known books', this refers to accounts in renowned Muslim traditions attributed to the sixth Imám, Ja'far-i-Ṣádiq, which relate how God told Noah to inform His followers that after eating dates they should plant the seeds and that once these grew to fruition, divine punishment would descend on their enemies. When the fresh fruits appeared, Noah was asked about the promised punishment; He said that God now wanted them to plant the seeds of this new fruit, and when they bore dates, then the punishment would come. As stated in the Íqán, this 'caused a few among the small number of His followers to turn away from Him'. The test according to the traditions was later repeated twice again with the same result. Finally God's command came to build the Ark which would protect all those who had persevered through the tests from the flood which would overtake the non-believers.

In the Persian Bayán the Báb explains that the non-fulfilment of a divine promise is another expression of God's power to do whatsoever He wills. No one can oppose this because His decree is just. Non-fulfilment when it concerns creation is related to weakness and limitation on the part of the creatures. But when it is attributed to God, it is evidence of His might and power.

7 **forty or seventy-two of His followers** The point is the fewness of Noah's followers after the trials described. Bahá'u'lláh here cites two different figures from the recorded traditions without giving a judgement as to which is the more accurate.

9 **Húd** First of the five Prophets of God mentioned in the Qur'án as having been sent to the peoples of

Arabia, which extended across the whole of the Arabian peninsula to the Sinai; the others are Ṣáliḥ, Abraham, Shu'ayb and Muḥammad. Húd came to the people of 'Ád; see Qur'án 7:65; 11:50–60; 26:123–40. 'Ád is known as the grandson of Aram, who was the grandson of Noah. Húd is possibly Eber of the Bible; see Genesis 10:24.

9 **For well-nigh seven hundred years** See note on nine hundred and fifty years at 7 above.

9 **Riḍván** Riḍván means Paradise and is also the name of the custodian of Paradise in Islamic traditions.

10 **Ṣáliḥ** The second of the five Prophets to the Arabs, in this case to the Thamúd tribe; some commentators identify Him with the Salah of Gen. 10:24. He is mentioned extensively in the Qur'án. According to Muslim traditions, Ṣáliḥ began His prophetic mission when He was 16, and lived for 120 years. When Ṣáliḥ was asked for a sign by the people who opposed Him, God sent them a She-Camel.[88] 'Abdu'l-Bahá explained that the She-Camel mentioned in relation to Ṣáliḥ's mission is a symbol of Ṣáliḥ Himself and the camel's offspring His blessed Faith.[89] In this sense Bahá'u'lláh addresses one of His enemies saying, that because of him 'the She-Camel was hamstrung'[90] and again, 'The heedless ones have hamstrung Thy white She-Camel, and caused Thy Crimson Ark to founder.'[91] In yet another passage He states: 'Consider the she-camel. Though but a beast, yet hath the All-Merciful exalted her to so high a station that the tongues of the earth made mention of her and celebrated her praise.'[92]

The old cemetery in 'Akká surrounds Ṣáliḥ's traditionally-accepted resting-place. It was in the shadow of His modest shrine that both Mírzá Miḥdí, the son of Bahá'u'lláh, and Navváb, Mírzá Mihdí's mother and Bahá'u'lláh's wife, were originally interred. Their remains have since been transferred to the Monument Gardens on Mount Carmel under the direction of Shoghi Effendi.

10 **city of God** See note at 218 below on **a thousand years**.

10 **Thamúd** The Thamúd tribe, or group of tribes, lived in northern Arabia, principally in al-Ḥijr, up to the southern border of Syria. They inhabited dwellings cut in the sides of mountains (Qur'án 7:74). Thamúdí inscriptions are found all over Arabia and indicate a unity of language and religion which suggests that once the tribe's authority extended further, especially in northern and central Arabia.

11 **Friend of God** Here a title of Abraham, the Father of the Faithful, Founder of the Jewish nation and an ancestor of Bahá'u'lláh, who is of His descent through Abraham's wife, Katurah. See 'Abdu'l-Bahá's account of Abraham in *Some Answered Questions*, chapter 4. See also numerous references in the Bible and the Qur'án. See also Íqán, para. 67.

11 **episode of the fire** 'Behold how the people, as a result of the verdict pronounced by the divines of His age, have cast Abraham, the Friend of God, into fire . . .'[93] It states in the Qur'án: 'They said, Burn him, and avenge your gods; if ye do this it will be well. And when Abraham was cast into the burning pile, we said, O fire, be thou cold, and a preservation unto Abraham.'[94] The traditions relate that 'by Nimrod's order, a large space was enclosed at Eritha and filled with a vast quantity of wood, which being set on fire burned so

fiercely that none dared venture near it: then they bound Abraham, and put him into an engine, shot him into the midst of the fire; from which he was preserved by the angel Gabriel who was sent to his assistance; the fire burning only the cords with which he was bound.'[95] He was delivered by divine intervention.[96]

11 **expelled from His city** Shoghi Effendi characterizes 'the banishment of Abraham from Ur of the Chaldees to the Promised Land – a banishment which, in the multitudinous benefits it conferred upon so many divers peoples, faiths and nations, constitutes the nearest historical approach to the incalculable blessings destined to be vouchsafed, in this day, and in future ages, to the whole human race, in direct consequence of the exile suffered by Him Whose Cause is the flower and fruit of all previous Revelations'.[97] The Old Testament refers to Ur of Chaldees as Abraham's native city[98] located in the region of Sumeria/ Mesopotamia, His banishment from there beginning, according to biblical and historical accounts, *circa* 1950 BC.

> 'Abdu'l-Bahá, after enumerating in His 'Some Answered Questions' the far-reaching consequences of Abraham's banishment, significantly affirms that 'since the exile of Abraham from Ur to Aleppo in Syria produced this result, we must consider what will be the effect of the exile of Bahá'u'lláh in His several removes . . .[99]

12 **Moses** He Who conversed with God and laid down the Ten Commandments; He Who delivered the Israelites from their exile in Pharaoh's Egypt and led them to the promised land of Israel. See Íqán paras. 57–58; also 'Abdu'l-Bahá's account in *Some Answered Questions*, chapter 5. See also numerous references in the Old Testament and the Qur'án.

12 **rod . . . white hand . . . serpent**   Terms used figuratively evoking the signs which Moses produced before Pharaoh and his court. 'So he threw his rod, then lo! it was a serpent manifest, and he drew forth his hand out of his bosom; and behold, it appeared white unto the spectators.'[100] 'White and splendid,' recounts an Islamic tradition, 'surpassing the brightness of the sun.' For the biblical version see Exodus 4:1–7. Bahá'u'lláh, with regard to Himself, later revealed: 'This is Mine hand which God hath turned white for all the worlds to behold. This is My staff; were We to cast it down, it would, of a truth, swallow up all created things.'[101]

12 **Párán**   A wilderness and a mountain between modern-day Israel and the Sinai peninsula, as in Genesis 21:21, Deuteronomy 33:2 and Habakkuk 3:3. 'References in the Bible to "Mt. Párán" and "Paraclete" refer to Muḥammad's Revelation.'[102]

12 **Sinai**   Mount Sinai, the principal site of Divine Revelation in Jewish history where Moses received the Ten Commandments. Usually identified as Jabal Músá, a massive granite pinnacle situated in the centre of the Sinai peninsula.

12 **Pharaoh**   Title of the ancient rulers of Egypt, the first dynasties of which are recorded *circa* 3100 BC. The Rameses dynasty encompassed the 14th and 13th centuries BC, the period of Moses. The Pharaohs were persecutors of Moses and His people. See also Íqán 12, 16, 57, 68, 92. Concerning the fierce opposition of Pharaoh see Exodus chapters 5 and 14. 'Abdu'l-Bahá affirms that

... the kingdom, wealth and power of Pharaoh and his people, which were the causes of the life of the nation, became, through their opposition, denial and pride, the cause of death, destruction, dispersion, degradation and poverty.[103]

12 **that blessed Tree . . . that sacred Tree** Moses Himself, i.e. the Manifestation of God symbolized as a Tree. See note on **hidden and sacred tree** at 22 below, and on **Sadratu'l-Muntahá** at 26 below.

12 **No earthly water . . . nor mortal blasts** Bahá'u'lláh further elaborates this theme in one of His prayers:

> I recognize, O Thou Who art my heart's Desire, that were fire to be touched by water it would instantly be extinguished, whereas the Fire which Thou didst kindle can never go out, though all the seas of the earth be poured upon it. Should water at any time touch it, the hands of Thy power would, as decreed in Thy Tablets, transmute that water into a fuel that would feed its flame.
>
> I, likewise, recognize, O my God, that every lamp, when exposed to the fury of the winds, must cease from burning. As to Thy Lamp, however, O Beloved of the worlds, I cannot think what power except Thy power could have kept it safe for so many years from the tempests that have continually been directed upon it by the rebellious among Thy creatures.[104]

As detachment is one of the requirements of the pathway of certitude, this image is also found in one of Bahá'u'lláh's prayers for detachment:

> Earth can never cloud its splendour, nor water quench its flame. All the peoples of the world are powerless to resist its force.[105]

12 **a believer of the kindred of Pharaoh** Said by some traditions to have been the son of Pharaoh's uncle. Several Qur'ánic commentators assume that this believer was the same person who warned Moses to flee after the latter had slain an Egyptian. See Qur'án 28:19 and following note.

12 **a shameful death** Accounts in traditions attributed to the Imáms state that Pharaoh's people cut this believer into pieces. The divine protection vouchsafed to him as mentioned in the Qur'án is understood to mean that God kept him firm in the face of martyrdom.

13 **all the Prophets . . . foretold the coming of yet another Prophet** 'Abdu'l-Bahá elaborates on this truth:

> . . . it is a basic principle of the Law of God that in every Prophetic Mission, He entereth into a Covenant with all believers – a Covenant that endureth until the end of that Mission, until the promised day when the Personage stipulated at the outset of the Mission is made manifest.[106]

14 **the motive for such deeds** In a similar vein, Bahá'u-'lláh writes:

> Thou hast known how grievously the Prophets of God, His Messengers and Chosen Ones, have been afflicted. Meditate a while on the motive and reason which have been responsible for such a persecution. At no time, in no Dispensation, have the Prophets of God escaped the blasphemy of their enemies, the cruelty of their oppressors, the denunciation of the learned of their age, who appeared in the guise of uprightness and piety. Day and night they passed through such agonies as none can ever measure, except the knowledge of the one true God, exalted be His glory.[107]

14 **To maintain that the testimony of Providence was incomplete** With regard to man's possibility of recognizing the verses of God which are revealed by every Prophet of God, Bahá'u'lláh explains that God has endowed every soul with 'the capacity' to recognize such signs. 'How could He, otherwise,' He adds, 'have fulfilled His testimony unto men, if ye be of them that ponder His Cause in their hearts. He will never deal unjustly with any one, neither will He task a soul beyond its power. He, verily, is the Compassionate, the All-Merciful.'[108]

14 **bounties . . . have, at all times . . . encompassed the earth** Bahá'u'lláh asks in one of His Tablets:

> What outpouring flood can compare with the stream of His all-embracing grace, and what blessing can excel the evidences of so great and pervasive a mercy? There can be no doubt whatever that if for one moment the tide of His mercy and grace were to be withheld from the world, it would completely perish. For this reason, from the beginning that hath no beginning the portals of Divine mercy have been flung open to the face of all created things, and the clouds of Truth will continue to the end that hath no end to rain on the soil of human capacity, reality and personality their favours and bounties. Such hath been God's method continued from everlasting to everlasting.[109]

14 **Sun of Truth** See Íqán, para. 31.

14 **weighed the testimony of God by the standard of their own knowledge** See note on **a standard** at 2 above. See also Íqán, para. 233.

15 **Leaders of religion, in every age, have hindered their people** Bahá'u'lláh expatiates on this theme in nu-

merous Tablets. In one, the Madínatu't-Tawḥíd (City of Unity) which, like the Íqán was revealed in Baghdád during the same period, we read:

> Consider the former generations. Witness how every time the Day Star of Divine bounty hath shed the light of His Revelation upon the world, the people of His Day have arisen against Him, and repudiated His truth. They who were regarded as the leaders of men have invariably striven to hinder their followers from turning unto Him Who is the Ocean of God's limitless bounty.

Then Bahá'u'lláh recapitulates in brief the afflictions of the past Prophets of God:

> Behold how the people, as a result of the verdict pronounced by the divines of His age, have cast Abraham, the Friend of God, into fire; how Moses, He Who held converse with the Almighty, was denounced as liar and slanderer. Reflect how Jesus, the Spirit of God, was, notwithstanding His extreme meekness and perfect tender-heartedness, treated by His enemies. So fierce was the opposition which He, the Essence of Being and Lord of the visible and invisible, had to face, that He had nowhere to lay His head. He wandered continually from place to place, deprived of a permanent abode. Ponder that which befell Muḥammad, the Seal of the Prophets, may the life of all else be a sacrifice unto Him. How severe the afflictions which the leaders of the Jewish people and of the idol-worshippers caused to rain upon Him, Who is the sovereign Lord of all, in consequence of His proclamation of the unity of God and of the truth of His Message![110]

15 **people of the Book**   Leaders of previous religions, namely the Jews and the Christians who opposed Muḥammad. The Qur'án condemns them for not accepting its truth and for trying to mislead the Mus-

lims. It further chides them for opposing each other while each possessed a Revelation from God, in the Torah and the Evangel. The leaders reject and vilify one another 'though they both recite the Book'.[111] Clearly, Muḥammad upheld the oneness and continuity of scripture.

The 'people of the Book' in a broader sense has been used by the Muslims to refer to followers in general of previous Revelations. Muḥammad Himself provided for the rights of Jews and Christians in Islamic society, allowing them places of worship and freedom to practise their faith. See also Íqán, para. 242.

16 **eye of God** The possibility of man seeing with the eye of God is affirmed in a number of passages in Bahá'u-'lláh's writings, for example:

> Open Thou, O my Lord, mine eyes and the eyes of all them that have sought Thee, that we may recognize Thee with Thine own eyes.[112]

> . . . look, then, upon Me with Mine own eyes, and not with the eyes of any one besides Me.[113]

> Thy sight is My sight, do thou see therewith . . .[114]

'Abdu'l-Bahá in a Tablet explains this arresting image:

> As to your question about the meaning of the Arabic Hidden Words: 'Couldst thou but see with Mine eye', when man reacheth the station of selflessness, and his love of self is entirely wiped out, his existence becometh like unto non-existence, and a ray from God's presence sheddeth its light upon him. Then he can see with the eye of God, and can hear with His ear. This is like iron in the fire. The qualities of the iron, its coldness, darkness and hardness are con-

cealed, and it manifests heat, luminosity and fluidity, which are the qualities of the fire.[115]

16 **Birds of Eternity** The Manifestations of God. See also Íqán, paras. 161, 190, 233, 283 and note on **Manifestations of God** at 3 above. Note in this passage the clearly stated principle that the Manifestations alone reveal the true meanings of the utterances of God. This reaffirms the biblical truth that scriptures are not open to 'private interpretation'.[116]

16 **Copt of tyranny** The term 'copt' refers to Pharaoh or the Egyptians, the Copts.

16 **Sept of justice** The term 'sept' is related to Moses or the Israelites; a sept is a division of a nation or a tribe.

16 **hand of the Moses of truth** See note on **the white hand** at 12 above.

16 '. . . **them that are well-grounded in knowledge**' A passage from the writings of the Báb explains this phrase in the following manner:

> Behold the learned who are honoured by virtue of their ability to understand the Holy Writings, and God hath exalted them to such a degree that in referring to them He saith: 'None knoweth the meaning thereof except God and them that are well-grounded in knowledge.'[117]

See also Íqán, para. 237.

17 **Jesus . . . protest against Him** 'Abdu'l-Bahá has summarized the objections of Israel and offers an explanation of the misunderstood prophecies:

When Christ appeared, twenty centuries ago, although the Jews were eagerly awaiting His Coming, and prayed every day, with tears, saying: 'O God, hasten the Revelation of the Messiah', yet when the Sun of Truth dawned, they denied Him and rose against Him with the greatest enmity, and eventually crucified that divine Spirit, the Word of God, and named Him Beelzebub, the evil one, as is recorded in the Gospel. The reason for this was that they said: 'The Revelation of Christ, according to the clear text of the Torah, will be attested by certain signs, and so long as these signs have not appeared, whoso layeth claim to be a Messiah is an impostor. Among these signs is this, that the Messiah should come from an unknown place, yet we all know this man's house in Nazareth, and can any good thing come out of Nazareth? The second sign is that He shall rule with a rod of iron, that is, He must act with the sword, but this Messiah has not even a wooden staff. Another of the conditions and signs is this: He must sit upon the throne of David and establish David's sovereignty. Now, far from being enthroned, this man has not even a mat to sit on. Another of the conditions is this: the promulgation of all the laws of the Torah; yet this man has abrogated these laws, and has even broken the sabbath day, although it is the clear text of the Torah that whosoever layeth claim to prophethood and revealeth miracles and breaketh the sabbath day, must be put to death. Another of the signs is this, that in His reign justice will be so advanced that righteousness and well-doing will extend from the human even to the animal world – the snake and the mouse will share one hole, and the eagle and the partridge one nest, the lion and the gazelle shall dwell in one pasture, and the wolf and the kid shall drink from one fountain. Yet now, injustice and tyranny have waxed so great in His time that they have crucified Him! Another of the conditions is this, that in the days of the Messiah the Jews will prosper and triumph over all the peoples of the world, but now they are living in the utmost abasement and servitude in the empire of the Romans. Then how can this be the

Messiah promised in the Torah?'

In this wise did they object to that Sun of Truth, although that Spirit of God was indeed the One promised in the Torah. But as they did not understand the meaning of these signs, they crucified the Word of God. Now the Bahá'ís hold that the recorded signs did come to pass in the Manifestation of Christ, although not in the sense which the Jews understood, the description in the Torah being allegorical. For instance, among the signs is that of sovereignty. For Bahá'ís say that the sovereignty of Christ was a heavenly, divine, everlasting sovereignty, not a Napoleonic sovereignty that vanisheth in a short time. For well nigh two thousand years this sovereignty of Christ hath been established, and until now it endureth, and to all eternity that Holy Being will be exalted upon an everlasting throne.

In like manner all the other signs have been made manifest, but the Jews did not understand. Although nearly twenty centuries have elapsed since Christ appeared with divine splendour, yet the Jews are still awaiting the coming of the Messiah and regard themselves as true and Christ as false.[118]

* 17 **Bible**   Here meaning the Hebrew Bible, the Old Testament.

17 **spirit of faith**   'Abdu'l-Bahá states:

> The fourth degree of spirit is the heavenly spirit; it is the spirit of faith and the bounty of God; it comes from the breath of the Holy Spirit, and by the divine power it becomes the cause of eternal life. It is the power which makes the earthly man heavenly, and the imperfect man perfect.[119]

18 **Our former Tablets**   Such as the earlier Arabic *Javáhiru'l-Asrár* (Gems of Mystery) which the Universal House of Justice has described thus:

In this mighty epistle, within the space of about one
hundred pages, Bahá'u'lláh refers to the grievous
tribulation and adversities that He suffered at the
hand of the infidels; deplored the perversity of the
followers of past religions; elucidates the meaning of
the signs and prophecies concerning the advent of
the new Manifestation, including the meaning of the
passage in the Bible where it says: 'Heaven and earth
shall pass away but My word shall not pass away';
affirms the continuity of divine revelation; unfolds
the significance of such symbolic terms as 'the Day of
Judgement', 'the Balance', 'the Way', 'the resurrection
of the dead' and 'the identity of the Promised Qá'im
and the place from which He is expected to appear';
asserts the inevitability of heaven-sent trials and
describes the inner meaning of such terms as 'life and
death', 'attainment to the presence of God', 'the
valley of bewilderment', the 'station of self-surrender',
and 'the character and qualities of those who have
attained His Court'.[120]

Adib Taherzadeh notes:

The importance of this Tablet becomes apparent
when we note that its themes are similar to those of
the Kitáb-i-Íqán. Although less in compass, its subjects are those which Bahá'u'lláh has more fully
elaborated in that book. For example, He enumerates
in this Tablet a number of causes which have prevented the followers of all religions from recognizing
the next Manifestation of God; stipulates some of the
qualities which the seeker must possess in order to
find the truth; affirms that God is unknowable in His
Essence; asserts the unity of all His Messengers;
explains the meaning of such terms as the Day of
Judgement, resurrection, life, death and similar
terminologies mentioned in the Holy Books of the
past; interprets certain prophecies from the Old and
New Testaments, and elucidates passages from the
Qur'án and traditions of Islám which anticipate the
coming of the Qá'im and the advent of the Day of

God, identified by Bahá'u'lláh with the appearance
of 'Him Whom God shall make manifest'.[121]

18 **language of Ḥijáz . . . accents of Iráq** By the language
of Ḥijáz is understood Arabic; 'the accents of 'Iráq'
refers here to Persian as indicated by the shift in
language at this point in the text. The Mesopotamian
region of 'Iráq was at the time populated by a majority
of Persian S̲h̲í'ís because of the highly significant S̲h̲í'í
holy places located there. See note on **Ḥijáz** at 71
below.

20 **Dispensation of the Qur'án** This dispensation began
with the Ministry of the Qur'án's Author, Muḥammad
(*circa* 612 AD), and ended with the Declaration of the
Báb in 1844.

> The Sun of Truth, after the advent of Muḥammad,
> no longer shone from the Christian horizon. Islám
> was, from then until the Báb's advent, the Path of
> Truth.[122]

The Muslim calendar dates from 622 AD, ten years
after Muḥammad's advent at the time of the Hijra. See
comment on Hijra under **Baṭḥá unto Yat̲h̲rib** at 54
below.

20 **Muḥammad** Prophet of God, revealer of the Qur'án,
founder of Islám. Born August 570 AD, declared His
mission 613 AD, died 632 AD. Bahá'u'lláh refers to Him
as God's 'Well-Beloved One'.[123]

20 **mysteries of distinction and unity** The explanation
of these mysteries is a major theme of the Íqán; concerning 'distinction' see especially paras. 191–2, and for
'unity' paras. 161–2.

20 **answer to thy question** This question is not among the ones in the original letter of the uncle of the Báb. Bahá'u'lláh evidently addresses Himself to points raised in the conversations held before Ḥájí Mírzá Siyyid Muḥammad composed his letter.

22 **hidden and sacred Tree** 'Verily He is the Tree of Life that bringeth forth the fruits of God . . .'[124]

See also notes on **Sadratu'l-Muntahá** at 26 below and on **tree that belongeth neither to the East nor to the West** at 57 below.

22 **Baghdád, the 'Abode of Peace'** (Dár al-Salám) Of Baghdád Shoghi Effendi writes:

> . . . described in Islamic traditions as 'Ẓahru'l-Kúfih', designated for centuries as the 'Abode of Peace', and immortalized by Bahá'u'lláh as the 'City of God' . . . To that city the Qur'án had alluded as the 'Abode of Peace' to which God Himself 'calleth'. To it, in that same Book, further allusion had been made in the verse 'For them is a Dwelling of Peace with their Lord . . . on the Day whereon God shall gather them all together'. From it radiated, wave after wave, a power, a radiance and a glory which insensibly reanimated a languishing Faith, sorely-stricken, sinking into obscurity, threatened with oblivion. From it were diffused, day and night, and with ever-increasing energy, the first emanations of a Revelation which, in its scope, its copiousness, its driving force and the volume and variety of its literature, was destined to excel that of the Báb Himself. Above its horizon burst forth the rays of the Sun of Truth, Whose rising glory had for ten long years been overshadowed by the inky clouds of a consuming hatred, an ineradicable jealousy, an unrelenting malice. In it the Tabernacle of the promised 'Lord of Hosts' was first erected, and the foundations of the long-awaited Kingdom of the

'Father' unassailably established. Out of it went forth the earliest tidings of the Message of Salvation which, as prophesied by Daniel, was to mark, after the lapse of 'a thousand two hundred and ninety days' (1290 AH), the end of 'the abomination that maketh desolate'. Within its walls the 'Most Great House of God', His 'Footstool' and the 'Throne of His Glory', 'the Cynosure of an adoring world', the 'Lamp of Salvation between earth and heaven', the 'Sign of His remembrance to all who are in heaven and on earth', enshrining the 'Jewel whose glory hath irradiated all creation', the 'Standard' of His Kingdom, the 'Shrine round which will circle the concourse of the faithful' was irrevocably founded and permanently consecrated.[125]

'The Abode of Peace' was first adopted as a name for Baghdád by the Caliph al-Manṣúr when he rebuilt the ancient city in 762 AD. See also Íqán, para. 188.

22 **bread from heaven** See note on **bread** at 5 above. Rodwell, in his translation of the Qur'án, translated this metaphor as 'table' rather than 'bread', which tends to distance it from its religious tradition.

23 **Nightingale of Paradise will have winged its flight** The nightingale is often used to symbolize the Manifestation of God in the Bahá'í writings. Those few days when the divine Messenger is present on earth among men and revealing the divine verses are very precious and incomparable. Thus Bahá'u'lláh asserts:

> O Son of Spirit! The time cometh, when the nightingale of holiness will no longer unfold the inner mysteries and ye will all be bereft of the celestial melody and of the voice from on high.[126]

As to Paradise: It is a reality and there can be no doubt about it, and now in this world it is realized

through love of Me and My good-pleasure. Whosoever attaineth unto it God will aid him in this world
below, and after death He will enable him to gain
admittance into Paradise whose vastness is as that of
heaven and earth.[127]

23 **Whosoever wisheth, let him turn thereunto** This re-
calls the passage from Bahá'u'lláh's Tablet of Aḥmad:
'Whosoever desireth, let him turn aside from this
counsel and whosoever desireth let him choose the
path to his Lord.'[128] Man is always at liberty to exercise
his free will or choice in such matters.

24 **Mary** See note on **Mary** at 59 below.

24 **signs that must needs herald the advent**

Now as regards the signs that would herald the
advent of the new Manifestation. The Guardian
wishes you to read over very carefully Bahá'u'lláh's
explanation as recorded in the Íqán. There it is made
clear that what is meant by the appearance of the Son
of God after the calamitous events preceding His
coming is the revelation of His full glory and its
recognition and acceptance by the peoples of the
world, and not his physical appearance. For Bahá'u-
'lláh, Whose advent marks the return of the Son in
the Glory of the Father, has already appeared, and
fulfilment, however, would mark the beginning of the
recognition of His full station by the peoples of the
world. Then and only then will His appearance be
made completely manifest.[129]

24 **in the three other Gospels** See Luke 21:25–8, Mark
13:24–7 and John 16:20.

24 **Our Tablets revealed in the Arabic tongue** See note
on **Our former Tablets** at 18 above.

25 **Christian divines**

> It seems both strange and pitiful that the Church and
> clergy should always, in every age, be the most bitter
> opponents of the very Truth they are continually
> admonishing their followers to be prepared to re-
> ceive! They have become so violently attached to the
> form that the substance itself eludes them!
>
> However, such denunciations as those your
> minister made publicly against you and the Bahá'í
> Faith can do no harm to the Cause at all; on the
> contrary they only serve to spread its name abroad
> and mark it as an independent religion.[130]

25 **following the example of the leaders of their faith**

> It is recorded in a tradition that of the entire con-
> course of the Christians no more than seventy people
> embraced the Faith of the Apostle of God. The blame
> falleth upon their doctors, for if these had believed,
> they would have been followed by the mass of their
> countrymen. Behold, then, that which hath come to
> pass! The learned men of Christendom are held to
> be learned by virtue of their safeguarding the teach-
> ing of Christ, and yet consider how they themselves
> have been the cause of men's failure to accept the
> Faith and attain unto salvation![131]

25 **Muḥammadan Dispensation** See note on **Dispensation of the Qur'án** at 20 above.

25 **Kawthar** Literally, 'abundance'; traditionally, a river
in Paradise whence all other rivers derive their source.
Often in the writings of Bahá'u'lláh this term has been
translated as a 'heavenly river' or a 'living fountain'
and similar phrases. For example, in the Long Obligatory Prayer, 'Make my prayer, O my Lord, a fountain
[Kawthar] of living waters whereby I may live as long
as Thy sovereignty endureth'.[132]

According to a tradition of the prophet's, this river, wherein his Lord promised him abundant good, is sweeter than honey, whiter than milk, cooler than snow, and smoother than cream; its banks are of chrysolites, and the vessels to drink thereout of silver; and those who drink of it shall never thirst.[133]

See also Íqán, paras. 65, 81, 118, 129, 161, 239, 249.

26 **Sadratu'l-Muntahá** The Divine Lote Tree; the 'tree beyond which there is no passing', a title of Bahá'u'lláh cited by Shoghi Effendi in *God Passes By*, p. 94. Bahá'u-'lláh states in a Tablet, 'The Holy Tree [Sadrat] is, in a sense, the Manifestation of the one True God, exalted be He.' See the explanation in context in *Tablets of Bahá'u'lláh revealed after the Kitáb-i-Aqdas*, p. 137.

28 **essential and highest purpose in creation** The motive behind creation is said to centre on man's attainment to the bounties of divine unity and understanding. The true principle of divine unity as defined by Bahá'u'lláh corrects the erroneous beliefs of some of the Muslim mystics of the past who viewed themselves at times as an embodiment of the divine Essence itself. 'He is a true believer in Divine unity', Bahá'u'lláh asserts,

> who, far from confusing duality with oneness, refuseth to allow any notion of multiplicity to becloud his conception of the singleness of God, who will regard the Divine Being as One Who, by His very nature, transcendeth the limitations of numbers.[134]

And again, revealing another aspect of such divine unity, He states:

> The essence of belief in Divine unity consisteth in regarding Him Who is the Manifestation of God and Him Who is the invisible, the inaccessible, the un-

knowable Essence as one and the same. By this is meant that whatever pertaineth to the former, all His acts and doings, whatever He ordaineth or forbiddeth, should be considered, in all their aspects, and under all circumstances, and without any reservation, as identical with the Will of God Himself. This is the loftiest station to which a true believer in the unity of God can ever hope to attain.[135]

This point is further reinforced in one of the meditations of Bahá'u'lláh:

Thy unity is inscrutable, O my God, to all except them that have recognized Him Who is the Manifestation of Thy singleness and the Day-Spring of Thy oneness.[136]

With regard to divine understanding, see note on **true understanding** at 1 above.

28 **an empty name . . . a dead letter** Muḥammad Himself has prophesied such a condition:

A day shall be witnessed by My people whereon there will have remained of Islá naught but a name, and of the Qur'án naught but a mere appearance. The doctors of that age shall be the most evil the world hath ever seen. Mischief hath proceeded from them, and on them it will recoil.[137]

28 **'Urvatu'l-Vuthqá** Translated as the 'Sure Handle', the 'Firm Cord', it is in its broadest sense an allusion to the Cause of God. 'Abdu'l-Bahá states:

Know thou that the 'Sure Handle' mentioned from the foundation of the world in the Books, the Tablets and the Scriptures of old is naught else but the Covenant and the Testament.[138]

See Qur'án 2:257, in which Muḥammad states, 'Whoever shall deny Ṭághút [the Idol] and believe in God
– he will have taken hold on a strong handle that shall
not be broken . . .' In one of His prayers Bahá'u'lláh
invokes God to 'write us down with such of Thy servants as have repudiated the Idol (Mírzá Yaḥyá), and
firmly believed in Thee'.[139] See also Qur'án 31:21 and
Íqán, paras. 37, 226.

30 **want of capacity** How well this description of the lack
of capacity to acquire spiritual knowledge fits, for the
most part, the condition of humankind during the
century since the Call of Bahá'u'lláh was first raised.

31 **These Suns of Truth** This key passage and the subsequent paragraph eloquently set forth the fundamental
role and exalted station of the universal Manifestations
of God.

31 **Through Him all things live, move**

> . . . all else besides these Manifestations, live by the
> operation of their Will, and move and have their
> being through the outpourings of their grace.[140]

See also Íqán, para. 226.

32 **confined at times to specific designations**

> These attributes of God are not and have never been
> vouchsafed specially unto certain Prophets, and
> withheld from others.[141]

32 **Prophets of God** Used here to refer to those 'endowed
with constancy'. See note at 240 below.

33 **immaculate Souls** Reference to the twelve Imáms of Shí'í Islám, the 'lawful Successors' of Muḥammad.[142] The Bahá'í teachings uphold the validity of the Imamate, 'that divinely-appointed institution of whose most distinguished member the Báb Himself was a lineal descendant, and which continued for a period of no less than two hundred and sixty years to be the chosen recipient of the guidance of the Almighty and the repository of one of the two most precious legacies of Islám.'[143]

Concerning the Imáms, Bahá'u'lláh Himself affirms, 'They, verily, are the manifestations of the power of God, and the sources of His authority, and the repositories of His knowledge, and the daysprings of His commandments.'[144]

Regarding the two legacies see Íqán, para. 222.

33 **Prayer of Nudbih** Famous prayer in Shí'í books which gives an account of the lives of all the Imáms and extols particularly the qualities of the Hidden Imám. Sometimes mistakenly attributed to the Imám 'Alí whose death, however, is described in it. Nudbih means 'lamentation'; in Arabic, the Wailing Wall in Jerusalem is called the Wall of Nudbih. See also Íqán, para. 269.

33 **'Whither are gone the resplendent Suns?'** Words of the Imám Mihdí, in the Prayer of Nudbih.

34 **Whosoever among the divines** While in the Íqán Bahá'u'lláh condemns the blindness and perversity of the divines, yet He extols the rank of those who are truly learned and who recognize the truth and light of succeeding Manifestations:

> Great is the blessedness of that divine that hath not allowed knowledge to become a veil between him and the One Who is the Object of all knowledge, and who,

when the Self-Subsisting appeared, hath turned with a beaming face towards Him. He, in truth, is numbered with the learned. The inmates of Paradise seek the blessing of his breath, and his lamp sheddeth its radiance over all who are in heaven and on earth. He, verily, is numbered with the inheritors of the Prophets. He that beholdeth him hath, verily, beheld the True One, and he that turneth towards him hath, verily, turned towards God, the Almighty, the All-Wise.[145]

36 **no doubt familiar with the interpretation** The interpretation of this verse current among the Shí'ís and based on Islamic tradition, namely from the Imám Riḍá, identifies the 'sun' and the 'moon' as referring to the first two Caliphs, Abú Bakr and 'Umar.

37 **'Urvatu'l-Vuthqá** See note at 28 above.

38 **laws of prayer and fasting** The term translated as 'prayer' in this and the following passages refers to that category of prayer which is obligatory in character rather than supplications in general. With reference to these two laws, Shoghi Effendi states:

> As regards fasting, it constitutes, together with the obligatory prayers, the two pillars that sustain the revealed Law of God. They act as stimulants to the soul, strengthen, revive and purify it, and thus insure its steady development.[146]

38 **lights that have emanated from the Day-Star of Truth** Reference to the Imáms; see note on **immaculate Souls** at 33 above.

39 **the law of prayer** 'Abdu'l-Bahá elucidates the importance of the station appointed for this law when with regard to the Bahá'í obligatory prayers He comments:

Through such prayer man holdeth communion with God, seeketh to draw near unto Him, converseth with the true Beloved of one's heart, and attaineth spiritual stations.[147]

Shoghi Effendi states that 'the obligatory prayers are by their very nature of greater effectiveness and are endowed with a greater power than the non-obligatory ones, and as such are essential.'[148]

40 **'Fasting is illumination, prayer is light.'**   A Sunní tradition attributed to Muḥammad.

40 **One day, a well known divine came**   This passage gives a first-hand account by Bahá'u'lláh Himself of His method of teaching and of the use of wisdom in conveying God's Word. See also Íqán, para. 186.

40 **Seal of the Prophets**   A title of Muḥammad.[149] In one sense it refers to His being the 'Seal' or the last of the Prophets (Nabiyyín) to announce the coming of the Day of God – the Day of the Báb and Bahá'u'lláh. As Bahá'u'lláh explains:

> This Day, however, is unique, and is to be distinguished from those that have preceded it. The designation 'Seal of the Prophets' fully revealeth its high station. The Prophetic Cycle hath, verily, ended. The Eternal Truth is now come.[150]

With the appearance of the Báb, the Prophetic Cycle which began with Adam drew to a close. See additional references, Íqán, paras. 172, 181, 196, 237.

40 **'Islám is heaven; fasting is its sun, prayer, its moon.'**   Muḥammad.

41 **camphor fountain** 'If the interpretation of "camphor" become known, the true intention will be evident.'[151] No further elucidation has been found in available Bahá'í writings. In the East, camphor is traditionally recognized as a powerful medicinal substance and mainly employed to subdue excessive carnal passion.

42 **would have surely comprehended the purpose of these terms** Bahá'u'lláh clarifies that their purpose is 'to test and prove the peoples of the world'.[152]

44 **the step of the spirit** Compare with this similar passage:

> O Son of Love! Thou art but one step away from the glorious heights above and from the celestial tree of love. Take thou one pace and with the next advance into the immortal realm and enter the pavilion of eternity. Give ear then to that which hath been revealed by the pen of glory.[153]

44 **swift as the twinkling of an eye** 'Be swift in the path of holiness, and enter the heaven of communion with Me.'[154] Also,

> This most great, this fathomless and surging Ocean is near, astonishingly near, unto you. Behold it is closer to you than your life-vein! Swift as the twinkling of an eye ye can, if ye but wish it, reach and partake of this imperishable favour, this God-given grace, this incorruptible gift, this most potent and unspeakably glorious bounty.[155]

44 **in one breath**

> These journeys have no visible ending in the world of time, but the severed wayfarer – if invisible confirmation descend upon him and the Guardian of the

Cause assist him – may cross these seven stages in seven steps, nay rather in seven breaths, nay rather in a single breath, if God will and desire it.[156]

46 **'cleaving of the heaven'** Cf. Isaiah 64:1, 'Oh that thou wouldest rend the heavens . . .'

48 **infinite knowledge . . . limited knowledge** This reference to two kinds of knowledge is further developed in a subsequent passage in which the two are described as divine and satanic. See Íqán, paras. 76, 201.

48 **'Knowledge is a light . . .'** Muḥammad. Consider in reference to the seeker in the *Four Valleys*:

> This station conferreth the true standard of knowledge, and freeth man from tests. In this realm, to search after knowledge is irrelevant, for He hath said concerning the guidance of travellers on this plane, 'Fear God, and God will instruct thee.' And again: 'Knowledge is a light which God casteth into the heart of whomsoever He willeth.'
>
> Wherefore, a man should make ready his heart that it be worthy of the descent of heavenly grace, and that the bounteous Cup-Bearer may give him to drink of the wine of bestowal from the merciful vessel.[157]

This tradition is also cited in Íqán, para. 201.

50 **physical earth to be changed** Consider in this connection Bahá'u'lláh's declaration:

> Were ye to be fair in your judgement, ye would readily recognize how the realities of all created things are inebriated with the joy of this new and wondrous Revelation, how all the atoms of the earth have been illuminated through the brightness of its glory.[158]

54 **Qiblih** 'Point of Adoration'; direction towards which the faithful turn in prayer. In Islám the Qiblih was changed from Jerusalem to Mecca. The original Qiblih mentioned in this paragraph was the house of worship, the Holy of Holies, built by the Israelites in Jerusalem and which became the centre of Jewish worship. The faithful used to turn towards it when offering their prayers. It remained the direction of prayer from the days after Moses and during the time of Christ, until it was altered by Muḥammad at the command of God. The Báb again changed the Qiblih by appointing 'Him Whom God shall make manifest' as the point of adoration. This point of prayer was to move with Him, in other words, with Bahá'u'lláh, until His passing, and then be fixed at His resting-place, His holy Shrine. Bahá'u'lláh confirmed this law in the Kitáb-i-Aqdas, the Most Holy Book, and after His Ascension, the Qiblih of the Bahá'í world became fixed at Bahjí.

54 **Baṭḥá unto Yathrib** A reference to Muḥammad's Hijra (Emigration) from Mecca to Medina in AD 622, in the fifty-third year of His life. 'Abdu'l-Bahá states that: 'The departure of Muḥammad, the Beloved of God, from the city of His birth was the cause of the exaltation of God's Holy Word . . .'[159]

The meaning of hijra is less geographical transference than separation and severance from family and kin. Baṭḥá is the central quarter and lowest part of Mecca which lies in a hollow close around the Ka'bih – Islám's most sacred shrine. It was inhabited by the ten main clans of the Quraysh, the aristocracy of the oldest families. Shortly after Muḥammad reached Yathrib, its name was changed to the 'City of the Prophet', al-Madínah an-Nabí. This was later abbreviated to al-Madínah or Medina in English usage. See note on **Mecca and Medina** at 93 below.

54 **Rik'at** Prostration; more generally, it refers to one complete Muslim devotional unit, which includes standing upright, bowing, prostrating and sitting. The whole forms a basic element of Muslim obligatory prayer.

54 **Gabriel** Archangel; considered in Islám as the mediator of revelation to Muḥammad and the person-ification of the Divine Spirit to Him. It was while in the Cave of Hira, outside the holy city of Mecca, that Muḥammad first heard the voice of Gabriel, which bade Him 'Cry in the name of Thy Lord.'[160] See also Íqán, paras. 92, 123, 174. According to the Bahá'í teachings, Gabriel, the 'Dove' and the 'Maid of Heaven' are symbols of the divine Reality of the Mani-festation Himself. 'Abdu'l-Bahá states clearly that the independent Prophets receive the bounty of divinity without any 'intermediary'.[161]

54 **Ka'bih** Literally, 'cube'. The cube-like building in the centre of the sacred Mosque at Mecca, which contains the Black Stone. It was founded by Abraham and remains the most holy shrine of Islám.

55 **David** Messenger of God, son of Jesse and second King of Israel; revealer of the Psalms. He rather than Saul was founder of the Jewish monarchy.[162]

55 **a particular purpose** As stated here, all the face of the earth is the same in the sight of God with the excep-tion of those places singled out by the Manifestations of God. Physically, these sites, these temples and holy houses, both during and after their relationship to God's Messengers, are the same. Shoghi Effendi, in a letter written on his behalf, has stated in a similar

connection with regard to the physical remains of the Manifestations:

> The atoms of the Prophets are just atoms, like all others, but the association of this great spiritual power with them leaves in the place they are laid to rest a spiritual atmosphere, if one can use this expression. They are, no doubt, endowed with a tremendous spiritual influence and far-reaching power. But the physical character of their atoms are not different from other people's, any more than their bodies and physical functions are different.[163]

56 **prison-cage of self and desire** See *Hidden Words*, Persian, no. 38.

57 **thus consume every intervening veil with the fire** See Íqán, paras. 19, 31, 205, 226.

57 **'Imrán** (Amran) His descendants include Moses and Aaron and they constitute a subdivision of the priestly Levites; not literally the father of Moses.

57 **To this testifieth the record of the sacred Book** See Exodus 2:12.

57 **Midian** A district on the eastern side of the Gulf of Aqaba extending north to the mountains east of the Dead Sea and west into the Sinai peninsula, occupied by the descendants of Midian, son of Abraham and Keturah. See Qur'án 7:83 and Genesis 25:2.

57 **Shoeb** (Shu'ayb) The Messenger of God sent to the Arab people of Midian. See Qur'án 7:85–93; 11:84–95. For His relationship to Moses, who became His son-in-law, see Qur'án 28:22–8. Identified in the Old Testament with Jethro, the priest of Midian (Exodus 3:1) or with Reuel (Exodus 2:18).

57 **holy vale** Of Towa, the place of Moses' revelation. Referred to frequently by Bahá'u'lláh,[164] most dramatically in the description of the activity taking place in this Day in that spot to be found in Bahá'u'lláh's Tablet to Czar Alexander II:

> He Who is the Father is come, and the Son (Jesus Christ), in the holy vale, crieth out: 'Here am I, here am I, O Lord, my God!', whilst Sinai circleth round the House, and the Burning Bush calleth aloud: 'The All-Bounteous is come mounted upon the clouds! Blessed is he that draweth nigh unto Him, and woe betide them that are far away.'[165]

57 **King of glory** Eventually, one of the titles of Bahá'u-'lláh Himself.[166]

57 **Tree that belongeth neither to the East nor to the West** The image of the Tree of Divine Revelation is derived from the Qur'ánic passage:

> God is the light of heaven and earth: the similitude of His light is a niche in a wall, wherein a lamp is placed, and the lamp enclosed in a case of glass; the glass appears as if it were a shining star. It is lighted with the oil of a Blessed Tree, an olive neither of the East, nor of the West; it wanteth little but that the oil thereof would give light, although no fire touched it. This is the light added unto light. God will direct unto His light whom He pleaseth.[167]

Shoghi Effendi elaborates on this theme, stating:

> Then, and only then, will the vast, the majestic process, set in motion at the dawn of the Adamic cycle, attain its consummation – a process which commenced six thousand years ago, with the planting, in the soil of the divine will, of the tree of divine revelation, and which has already passed through

certain stages and must needs pass through still others ere it attains its final consummation. The first part of this process was the slow and steady growth of this tree of divine revelation, successively putting forth its branches, shoots and offshoots, and revealing its leaves, buds and blossoms, as a direct consequence of the light and warmth imparted to it by a series of progressive dispensations associated with Moses, Zoroaster, Buddha, Jesus, Muḥammad and other Prophets, and of the vernal showers of blood shed by countless martyrs in their path. The second part of this process was the fruition of this tree, 'that belongeth neither to the East nor to the West', when the Báb appeared as the perfect fruit and declared His mission in the Year Sixty in the city of Shíráz.[168]

57 **from the valley of self and desire . . . attain . . . heavenly delight** Consider in light of the opening comments of the *Seven Valleys*:

> The stages that mark the wayfarer's journey from the abode of dust to the heavenly homeland are said to be seven . . . And they say that until the wayfarer taketh leave of self, and traverseth these stages, he shall never reach to the ocean of nearness and union, nor drink of the peerless wine.[169]

57 **Salsabíl** The name of 'a heavenly river' or 'wellspring' in Paradise; it implies easy, sweet, soft-flowing waters. See Qur'án 76:18.

57 **the peaceful city** 'Daru'l-Salám' See note on **Baghdad, the 'Abode of Peace'** at 22 above.

59 **Mary** The Virgin Mary, mother of Jesus Christ. The characterization of the Mother of Jesus throughout this passage has been singled out as one of the major themes of the Íqán by Shoghi Effendi when, in summarizing the text, he states that the Íqán 'upholds the

purity and innocence of the Virgin Mary'.[170] Refer to section 3 above. Compare *Promised Day is Come*, where Mary is described as 'that veiled and immortal, that most beauteous, countenance'.[171] See Íqán, paras. 24, 88, 141, 144, 191. See also note on **Fáṭimih** at 178 below.

59 a Babe Whose father was unknown

> With regard to your question concerning the Virgin Birth of Jesus; on this point, as on several others, the Bahá'í teachings are in full agreement with the doctrines of the Catholic Church. In the Kitáb-i-Íqán (Book of Certitude) page 56, and in a few other Tablets still unpublished, Bahá'u'lláh confirms, however indirectly, the Catholic conception of the Virgin Birth. Also 'Abdu'l-Bahá in 'Some Answered Questions', Chap. 12, page 73, explicitly states that Christ found existence through the spirit of God which statement necessarily implies, when reviewed in the light of the text, that Jesus was not the son of Joseph.[172]

> First regarding the birth of Jesus Christ. In the light of what Bahá'u'lláh and 'Abdu'l-Bahá have stated concerning this subject it is evident that Jesus came into this world through the direct intervention of the Holy Spirit, and that consequently His birth was quite miraculous. This is an established fact, and the friends need not feel at all surprised, as the belief in the possibility of miracles has never been rejected in the Teachings. Their importance, however, has been minimized.[173]

> What science calls a virgin birth we do not associate with that of Jesus Christ, which we believe to have been a miracle and a sign of His Prophethood. In this matter we are in entire agreement with the most orthodox church views.[174]

It would be sacrilege for a Bahá'í to believe that the parents of Jesus were illegally married and that the latter was consequently of an illegal union. Such a possibility cannot be even conceived by a believer who recognizes the high station of Mary and the Divine Prophethood of Jesus Christ. It is this same false accusation which the people of His Day attributed to Mary that Bahá'u'lláh indirectly repudiated in the Íqán. The only alternative therefore is to admit that the birth of Jesus has been miraculous. The operation of miracles is not necessarily irrational or illogical. It does by no means constitute a limitation of the Omnipotence of God. The belief in the possibilities of miracles, on the contrary, implies that God's power is beyond any limitation whatsoever. For it is only logical to believe that the Creator, Who is the sole Author of all the laws operating in the universe, is above them and can, therefore, if He deems it necessary, alter them at His Own Will. We, as humans, cannot possibly attempt to read His Mind, and to fully grasp His Wisdom. Mystery is therefore an inseparable part of true religion, and as such, should be recognized by the believers.[175]

Again with regard to your question relative to the birth of Jesus; he wishes me to inform you that there is nothing further he can add to the explanation he gave you in his previous communication regarding this point. One thing, however, he wishes again to bring to your attention, namely that miracles are always possible, even though they do not constitute a regular channel whereby God reveals His power to mankind. To reject miracles on the ground that they imply a breach of the laws of nature is a very shallow, well-nigh a stupid argument, inasmuch as God Who is the Author of the universe can, in His Wisdom and Omnipotence, bring any change, no matter how temporary, in the operation of the laws which He Himself has created.

The Teachings do not tell us of any miraculous birth besides that of Jesus.[176]

The Master clearly writes in a Tablet that Christ was *not* begotten in the ordinary way, but by the Holy Spirit. So we must accept this. Every Faith has some miracles, and this is the great miracle of the Christian Faith. But we must not let it be a test to us. Our human minds are so small, and as yet so immature compared to the men of the future, that we should have no difficulty in acknowledging the Power of God when He chooses to show it in some manner 'illogical' to us![177]

59 **return unto her home** In other words, to Nazareth.

59 **O sister of Aaron** Reference to Mary, the mother of Jesus. Aaron, the brother of Moses and his senior by three years, was a Levite descended from 'Imrán (Amran). The priestly class of Judaism are his descendants. Mary was of this class, hence she is addressed in the Qur'án 19:28, 'O sister of Aaron'. She is said to have been devoted to Temple service between the ages of three and twelve years. The term 'sister' is used here in a broad sense to denote Mary's lineal relationship to Aaron.

63 **How grievous the charges** Bahá'u'lláh Himself elaborates on these charges:

No sooner did He reveal Himself, than all the people rose up against Him. By some He was denounced as one that hath uttered slanders against God, the Almighty, the Ancient of Days. Others regarded Him as a man smitten with madness, an allegation which I, Myself, have heard from the lips of one of the divines. Still others disputed His claim to be the Mouthpiece of God, and stigmatized Him as one who had stolen and used as his the words of the Almighty, who had perverted their meaning, and mingled them with his own. The Eye of Grandeur weepeth sore for the things which their mouths have uttered, while they continue to rejoice upon their seats.[178]

63 **How severe the persecutions** Shoghi Effendi summarizes the calamities meted out to the Báb:

> Sudden arrest and confinement in the very first year of His short and spectacular career; public affront deliberately inflicted in the presence of the ecclesiastical dignitaries of S͟híráz; strict and prolonged incarceration in the bleak fastnesses of the mountains of Ád͟hirbáyján; a contemptuous disregard and a cowardly jealousy evinced respectively by the Chief Magistrate of the realm and the foremost minister of his government; the carefully staged and farcical interrogatory sustained in the presence of the heir to the Throne and the distinguished divines of Tabríz; the shameful infliction of the bastinado in the prayer house, and at the hands of the S͟hayk͟hu'l-Islám of that city; and finally suspension in the barrack-square of Tabríz and the discharge of a volley of above seven hundred bullets at His youthful breast under the eyes of a callous multitude of about ten thousand people, culminating in the ignominious exposure of His mangled remains on the edge of the moat without the city gate – these were the progressive stages in the tumultuous and tragic ministry of One Whose age inaugurated the consummation of all ages, and Whose Revelation fulfilled the promise of all Revelations.[179]

64 **the sweet savours of God were being wafted** This and the following paragraph clearly foreshadow the impending Declaration of Bahá'u'lláh's Own prophetic mission. His soul laden with the divine riches accumulating since the intimation of that mission, first communicated to Him in 1852 in the darkness of the underground dungeon of the Síyáh- C͟hál of Ṭihrán, here pours forth some of the mysteries of its hidden experience. The reader is permitted a glimpse of the inner workings of the latent splendours of His mighty

revelation, a revelation, which as characterized by
Shoghi Effendi, is 'hailed as the promise and crowning
glory of past ages and centuries, as the consummation
of all the Dispensations within the Adamic Cycle,
inaugurating an era of at least a thousand years'
duration, and a cycle destined to last no less than five
thousand centuries, signalizing the end of the Prophetic Era and the beginning of the Era of Fulfilment,
unsurpassed alike in the duration of its Author's
ministry and the fecundity and splendour of His
mission . . .'[180]

64 **Sheba of the Eternal** This allusion – coming as it does
in the middle of a passage very suggestive of Bahá'u-
'lláh's inherent but not yet fully disclosed divinity –
would seem to correspond to that inner dimension of
the Manifestation of God, that Divine effulgence from
God's Essence, which constitutes His eternal nature.

64 **the holy Spirit itself is envious!** In a similar mode
Bahá'u'lláh elsewhere proclaims: 'The Holy Spirit
Itself hath been generated through the agency of a
single letter revealed by this Most Great Spirit, if ye
be of them that comprehend.'[181] In the light of other
explanations this may be understood as a reference
to the greater magnitude of the one same Light which
shines from Bahá'u'lláh and which He was commissioned by God to reveal. The term 'Holy Spirit' is
often identified with Christ's Revelation and the 'Most
Great Spirit' with that of Bahá'u'lláh. The distinction
drawn here conforms to the principle of progressive
revelation.

65 **Kawthar** A river in paradise. See note at 25 above.

65 **Leviathan** An aquatic animal (real or imaginary) of enormous size. Figuratively, one of vast and formidable power.

65 **Phoenix** 'The Phoenix of the realms above crieth out from the immortal Branch: "The glory of all greatness belongeth to God, the Incomparable, the All-Compelling!"'[182] The *Oxford English Dictionary* defines the phoenix as 'A mythical bird, of gorgeous plumage, fabled to be the only one of its kind, and to live five or six hundred years in the Arabian desert, after which it burnt itself to ashes on a funeral pile of aromatic twigs ignited by the sun and fanned by its own wings, but only to emerge from its ashes with renewed youth, to live through another cycle of years.' Used figuratively for a person of unique excellence and beauty.

65 **guard it with the globe of understanding** Compare with Shoghi Effendi's statement that 'the greatest of all protections is knowledge'[183] and his note that 'it is better to have one Bahá'í who understands the Teachings and is wholeheartedly convinced of their truth, than a number of Bahá'ís, who are not well aware of the Cause, and deep-rooted in the Covenant.'[184]

66 **a star will appear** '. . . the Teachings bear no reference to the names of the stars which are supposed to have preceded Moses, Christ and other Divine Prophets.'[185]

66 **true and exalted Morn** Bahá'u'lláh states:

> O My servants! There shineth nothing else in Mine heart except the unfading light of the Morn of Divine guidance, and out of My mouth proceedeth naught but the essence of truth, which the Lord your God hath revealed.[186]

Further consider the following Hidden Word and its interpretation by 'Abdu'l-Bahá:

> O My Friends! Have ye forgotten that true and radiant morn, when in those hallowed and blessed surroundings ye were all gathered in My presence beneath the shade of the tree of life, which is planted in the all-glorious paradise? Awe-struck ye listened as I gave utterance to these three most holy words: O friends! Prefer not your will to Mine, never desire that which I have not desired for you, and approach Me not with lifeless hearts, defiled with worldly desires and cravings. Would ye but sanctify your souls, ye would at this present hour recall that place and those surroundings, and the truth of My utterance should be made evident unto all of you.[187]

> There are a few passages in *The Hidden Words* which refer implicitly to the Covenant of Bahá'u'lláh . . . 'Abdu'l-Bahá . . . has explained the meanings of some of these passages . . .
>   The 'true and radiant morn' . . . refers to the Revelation of the Báb, the 'tree of life' to Bahá'u'lláh, and the 'hallowed and blessed surroundings' to the heart of the individual. He further explained that the gathering referred to in this verse was not a physical but a spiritual one. The call of God was raised within the sanctuary of their hearts; but they did not respond and were bewildered and awestruck.[188]

67 **Nimrod dreamed a dream** Ancient king of Babylon; identified as the persecutor of Abraham in Islamic traditions. See Qur'án 2:260; 21:70. See note on **episode of the fire** at 11 above. In Bible dictionaries Nimrod (Powerful) son of Cush, son of Ham, son of Noah (Genesis 10:8–9), is described as a brave man, a hunter, a champion, governor of the world and the builder of Babylon. Babylon for some time was called the land of Nimrod. Islamic traditions state that

because he was nourished by a tigress at the order of God, he became known as Nimrod, as Nimrod means tigress in Arabic. The account of Nimrod and Abraham, and the throwing of the latter into the fire, have all been related by Majlisí in the fifth volume of the Biháru'l-Anvár. See note at 272 below.

Accounts of Nimrod's dream have been related in various books, including Qisasu'l-Anbíyá of Abú-Isháq Níshábúrí which states:

> Nimrod was told by the priests that in the coming two or three years a child will be separated from his mother and your sovereignty will be demolished by him. Nimrod ordered to kill every child who became separated from his mother. This order was carried out for three years.

It has been related that Nimrod had a terrible dream. He asked the wise men its interpretation. In interpreting it, one of them announced to him the advent of Abraham. Some of the ancient accounts are contradictory in reporting this dream; one of them says that Nimrod's personal astrologer, Azar, dreamed the dream of his coming destruction. Majlisí relates in volume 14 of the Bihár from Káfí, that the Imám Ṣádiq has stated that this Azar was Abraham's father and was the private astrologer of Nimrod. One night Azar understood from the arrangement of the stars that a boy would appear in that land who would destroy Nimrod and his followers. In the morning he informed Nimrod about this matter and said to him that very soon the seed of this boy will be fixed in the womb of his mother. Nimrod was astonished and asked whether the boy was already in the womb of the mother. Azar answered that it was not yet, and that Nimrod could order that men not cohabit with their women. And so it was that no woman was allowed to be with husband.

But Azar himself slept with his wife and they themselves conceived Abraham. Azar, from the position of the stars, knew that they would burn his son but he did not know that God would save him.

68 He Who held converse with God

Bahá'u'lláh is not the intermediary between other Manifestations and God. Each has His own relation to the Primal Source. But in the sense that Bahá'u-'lláh is the greatest Manifestation to yet appear, the One who consummates the Revelation of Moses, He was the One Moses conversed with in the Burning Bush. In other words, Bahá'u'lláh identifies the glory of the God-Head on that occasion with Himself. No distinction can be made amongst the Prophets in the sense that They all proceed from one Source, and are of one essence. But Their stations and functions in this world are different.[189]

69 Magi Members of the ancient Persian priestly caste of the Zoroastrian Faith; the 'wise men' who brought offerings to the infant Jesus.

69 Herod King of Judaea, known as Herod I, the Great; ordered the slaughter of infant boys around the time of the birth of Christ.

Consider and call thou to mind the days whereon the Spirit of God (Jesus Christ) appeared, and Herod gave judgement against Him. God, however, aided Him with the hosts of the unseen, and protected Him with truth, and sent Him down unto another land, according to His promise. He, verily, ordaineth what He pleaseth.[190]

Not to be confused with his son, Herod Antipas, who was responsible for beheading John the Baptist.

69 **the city which was the seat of the Kingdom of Herod**
Jerusalem.

70 **Yaḥyá** Yaḥyá is Arabic for John and here refers to
John the Baptist, son of Zachariah.

70 **Zachariah** Father of John the Baptist; of priestly
descent from Aaron.

70 **John the Baptist** Divinely-appointed forerunner of
Jesus Christ. Of priestly descent, his mother was cousin
of the Virgin Mary. He baptized Jesus and was beheaded by Herod Antipas.[191]

> They that have turned aside from Me have spoken
> even as the followers of John (the Baptist) spoke. For
> they, too, protested against Him Who was the Spirit
> (Jesus) saying: 'The dispensation of John hath not yet
> ended; wherefore hast thou come?'[192]

> John appeared before Jesus, proclaiming his [John's]
> prophethood, and all sects of Islám recognize him as
> a prophet; and he came with laws and command-
> ments . . .[193]

> This Manifestation and that of the Point of the Bayán
> [the Báb] are exactly similar to that of the son of
> Zachariah [John] and Jesus, the Son of Mary.[194]

71 **Rúz-bih** A Persian of Zoroastrian parents who embraced Christianity and who, after being told of the
Prophet's coming by the four heralds of Muḥammad,
journeyed to Arabia, attained His presence, and
recognized Him. After his conversion he became
known as Salmán, the Persian.

71 **Ḥijáz** A region in southwestern Arabia considered the
holy land of the Muslims. The sacred cities of Mecca

and Medina and many other places connected with the history of Muḥammad are found there. The 'language of Ḥijáz', mentioned in the writings, is Arabic.

72 **appearance of its star**   In 1843, just prior to the Declaration of the Báb, a great comet suddenly appeared in the heavens:

> The *Comet of 1843* is regarded as perhaps the most marvellous of the present age, having been observed in the daytime even before it was visible at night – passing very near the sun, exhibiting an enormous length of tail; and arousing interest in the public mind as universal and deep as it was unprecedented.[195]

72 **twin resplendent lights**   Bahá'u'lláh later in His Ministry assigned this same designation 'Núrayn-i-Nayyiraya' to two famous brothers, Mírzá Muḥammad Ḥasan and Mírzá Muḥammad Ḥusayn, respectively surnamed the King of Martyrs and the Beloved of Martyrs, who in 1879 were killed in Iṣfáhán.

72 **Aḥmad** (Shaykh Aḥmad-i-Aḥsá'í)   The first of the 'twin resplendent lights' who heralded the Báb and Bahá'u'lláh; founder of the Shaykhí movement; author of numerous religious writings. Died in 1826; buried in Medina.

> The followers of Shaykh-i-Aḥsá'í (Shaykh Aḥmad) have, by the aid of God, apprehended that which was veiled from the comprehension of others, and of which they remained deprived.[196]

72 **Kázim** (Siyyid Kázim-i-Rashtí)   The second of the 'twin resplendent lights' who heralded the Báb and Bahá'u'lláh. He was the chief disciple of Shaykh Aḥmad and his successor. He died at Karbilá on 31 December 1843.

74 descended from the heaven of the will of God

The Prophets, unlike us, are pre-existent. The soul
of Christ existed in the spiritual world before His
birth in this world. We cannot imagine what that
world is like, so words are inadequate to picture His
state of being.[197]

74 true habitations

They imagine that Christ was excluded from His
heaven in the days when He walked the earth, that
He fell from the heights of His sublimity, and afterwards mounted to those upper reaches of the sky, to
the heaven which doth not exist at all, for it is but
space.[198]

74 'Nothing whatsoever keepeth Him . . .' An Arabic
verse of Bahá'u'lláh Himself.

75 heaven Bahá'u'lláh cites here the names of distinct
heavens, indicating that each has a special meaning.
While not revealing the intention of these heavens,
each is related to terms that to some extent are defined by other passages in the Bahá'í writings. An
examination of these terms helps us to understand
something of their meaning in the context of this
passage.

75 'heaven' hath been applied to many and divers things
For one of these diverse applications consider the use
of the term 'heaven' in the following passage from
Bahá'u'lláh:

If the whole earth were to be converted into silver
and gold, no man who can be said to have truly
ascended into the heaven of faith and certitude would
deign to regard it, much less to seize and keep it.[199]

And again,

> He it is Who hath unveiled to your eyes the treasures
> of His knowledge, and caused you to ascend unto the
> heaven of certitude – the certitude of His resistless,
> His irrefutable, and most exalted Faith.[200]

75 **'The names come down from heaven'**   A Persian
proverb.

76 **Knowledge**   This passage clearly extols that knowledge
which is divine in origin and condemns that which
arises from the self of man. Human learning can act
as a terrible veil blinding the soul to its purpose in life
and its ultimate destiny. Useful knowledge acquired
in conformity with the bidding of the Prophets of God
is, however, most praiseworthy. As Bahá'u'lláh indicates:

> Arts, crafts and sciences uplift the world of being,
> and are conducive to its exaltation. Knowledge is as
> wings to man's life, and a ladder for his ascent. Its
> acquisition is incumbent upon everyone . . . In truth,
> knowledge is a veritable treasure for man, and a
> source of glory, of bounty, of joy, of exaltation, of
> cheer and gladness unto him. Happy the man that
> cleaveth unto it, and woe betide the heedless.[201]

While Bahá'u'lláh extols the study of sciences and arts,
He directs man to 'such sciences as are useful and
would redound to the progress and advancement of
the people'.[202] The point to bear in mind with regard
to the acquisition of knowledge and education is that
it must not be allowed to become a barrier between
oneself and God. 'Abdu'l-Bahá emphasizes this truth
as follows:

> Although to acquire the sciences and arts is the

greatest glory of mankind, this is so only on condition that man's river flow into the mighty sea, and draw from God's ancient source His inspiration. When this cometh to pass, then every teacher is as a shoreless ocean, every pupil a prodigal fountain of knowledge. If, then, the pursuit of knowledge lead to the beauty of Him Who is the Object of all Knowledge, how excellent that goal; but if not, a mere drop will perhaps shut a man off from flooding grace, for with learning cometh arrogance and pride, and it bringeth on error and indifference to God.

The sciences of today are bridges to reality; if then they lead not to reality, naught remains but fruitless illusion. By the one true God! If learning be not a means of access to Him, the Most Manifest, it is nothing but evident loss.

It is incumbent upon thee to acquire the various branches of knowledge, and to turn thy face toward the beauty of the Manifest Beauty, that thou mayest be a sign of saving guidance amongst the peoples of the world, and a focal centre of understanding in this sphere from which the wise and their wisdom are shut out, except for those who set foot in the Kingdom of lights and become informed of the veiled and hidden mystery, the well-guarded secret.[203]

76 **Satanic** This term is used occasionally in the Bahá'í writings, most frequently in the Íqán. Satan refers not to an ultimate evil being but to the animal nature in the human being that is to be overcome. See *Some Answered Questions*, pp. 235–6 for 'Abdu'l-Bahá's description of the conflict between the 'divine power in man' and 'satanic power'.

76 **'Fear ye God; God will teach you.'** Qur'án 2:282.

76 **'Knowledge is the most grievous veil . . .'** A traditional Ṣúfí saying.

76 **'Cling unto the robe . . .'** From a poem of Ibn Fáriz of Egypt (1198 AD).

77 **'He that treadeth the snow-white Path . . .'** Abu'l-Ghádir Muhiy-i-Dín Gílání, in the Bisharitu'l-Khayrát.

78 **the garb of pilgrimage** The seeker on his quest for the inner meaning of the Word of God must 'don the garb of pilgrimage'. In Islám, the believers are called upon once in their lifetime to make a pilgrimage to Mecca and circle round the Ka'bih in the centre of the Holy Mosque, the Qiblih of the Muslim world. It is prescribed that the pilgrims replace their traditional dress with a very simple set of two pieces of unsewn white cloth. Thus the symbols of social, political and familial distinction are transcended and all approach their goal concentrating on those inner qualities of submission and humility which should characterize the pilgrimage. Similarly, in approaching the inner meaning of the divine verses, we are called upon to discard the trappings of worldly position, of acquired learning and the like.

78 **Ka'bih** The most holy shrine at Mecca. See note at 54 above.

80 **subject to poverty and afflictions**

> . . . we must remember that the Prophets of God Themselves were not immune from these things which men suffer. They knew sorrow, illness and pain too. They rose above these things through Their spirits, and that is what we must try and do too, when afflicted. The troubles of this world pass, and what we have left is what we have made of our souls; so it is to this we must look – to becoming more spiritual, drawing nearer to God, no matter what our human minds and bodies go through.[204]

80 **'But for Thee . . '** Ḥadíth-i-Qudsí of Muḥammad.

81 **Consider how men for generations have been blindly imitating their fathers** 'Abdu'l-Bahá describes blind imitation as the cause of prejudice:

> . . . the root cause of prejudice is blind imitation of the past – imitation in religion, racial attitudes, in national bias, in politics. So long as this aping of the past persisteth, just so long will the foundations of the social order be blown to the four winds, just so long will humanity be continually exposed to direst peril.[205]

81 **Salsabíl** The name of a fountain or river in Paradise. See note at 57 above.

81 **Kawthar** A river in paradise. See note at 25 above.

82 **recognize Him only by His own Self**

> The first and foremost testimony establishing His truth is His own Self. Next to this testimony is His Revelation. For whoso faileth to recognize either the one or the other He hath established the words He hath revealed as proof of His reality and truth.[206]

> He Who is everlastingly hidden from the eyes of men can never be known except through His Manifestation, and His Manifestation can adduce no greater proof of the truth of His Mission than the proof of His own Person.[207]

85 **sovereignty manifest in every land**

> How vast is the tabernacle of the Cause of God! It hath overshadowed all the peoples and kindreds of the earth, and will, ere long, gather together the whole of mankind beneath its shelter.[208]

86 angels

The meaning of 'angels' is the confirmations of God and His celestial powers. Likewise angels are blessed beings who have severed all ties with this nether world, have been released from the chains of self and the desires of the flesh, and anchored their hearts to the heavenly realms of the Lord. These are of the Kingdom, heavenly; these are of God, spiritual; these are revealers of God's abounding grace; these are dawning-points of His spiritual bestowals.[209]

We do not know the nature of these angelic beings. Sometimes it refers to individual departed souls, sometimes it means the Spirit of Bahá'u'lláh, sometimes it is used as a figure of speech.[210]

In another Tablet 'Abdu'l-Bahá addresses Mírzá Mihdí Akhaván-i-Safá with an explanation of the Qur'ánic verse referring to angels with two, three or four wings. The Master explains that by wings is meant the power of divine confirmation and assistance through which man is able to ascend to the zenith of true understanding and soar to the very heart of Paradise with a rapidity that no one can conceive. By angels is meant those holy realities which are aware of the grace of their Lord, sanctified from all deficiencies and evil tendencies, purified from defect, and have attained all goodly gifts. These are they who speak not till He hath spoken, and who act in accordance with the command of God.[211]

86 **Cherubim** Angelic beings, held traditionally by Christians to be of the second order of a ninefold celestial hierarchy and gifted with knowledge and wisdom. See also **Seraph of God** at 123 below.

86 **Ṣádiq** The sixth of the holy Imáms of Islám. Known also as Abú-Abdi'lláh.[212]

86 **philosopher's stone** The supreme object of alchemy; a substance supposed to have the power to transmute baser metals into gold or silver. Symbolically used to refer to anything extremely rare.

89 **Letters of Unity** Traditional reference to the twelve S͟hí'í Imáms. See note on **immaculate Souls** at 33 above.

89 **'Verily Our Word is abstruse . . .'** Muḥammad.

89 **'Our Cause is sorely trying . . .'** Muḥammad.

90 **Qá'im** The Promised One of S͟hí'í Islám whose coming is fulfilled in the appearance of the Báb. Literally, 'He Who Ariseth' from the family of Muḥammad. 'The Báb is the return of the 12th Imám only in a spiritual sense, just as Bahá'u'lláh is the return of the Spirit of Christ.'[213]

91 **Books . . . corrupted** The explanation which Bahá'u-'lláh gives of the meaning of the corruption or modification (taḥríf) of the text has particular significance for those of Islamic background. For as a result of the misinterpretation of certain Qur'ánic verses, the Muslims have gradually come to the belief that the existing texts of the Old and New Testaments are without value and have been corrupted beyond recognition. This point of view is forcefully countered by Bahá'u'lláh, who sets down the true meaning of a few instances where modification of the verses has been mentioned. In the story of Ibn-i-Ṣúríyá He explains the historical context for the Qur'ánic verse 4:45, 'They pervert the text of the Word of God.' By 'by corruption of the text', He then states, 'is meant . . . the interpretation of God's holy Book in accordance

with their idle imaginings and vain desires.' It does not mean the actual words of Revelation have been effaced. This is not to deny, however, questions related to attribution and authenticity of various biblical books and passages in modern scholarship. A further point made is that the divines and followers of these previous holy books would never have wittingly mutilated their own time-honoured scriptures.

Bahá'u'lláh has similarly warned the people of this day against corrupting the scriptures:

> Whoso interpreteth what hath been sent down from the heaven of Revelation, and altereth its evident meaning, he, verily, is of them that have perverted the Sublime Word of God, and is of the lost ones in the Lucid Book.[214]

92 **'Modification by the exalted beings' and 'alteration by the disdainful'** Words attributed to the Imáms.

92 **Ibn-i-Ṣúríyá** The rabbi chosen by the people of Khaybar at Muḥammad's request to cite a point of Jewish law.

92 **Khaybar** Name of a famous oasis and of its principal settlement almost a hundred miles north of Medina. It was heavily populated with wealthy Jewish farmers and merchants. See note on **Battle of Khaybar** at 179 below.

92 **by God Who clove the sea for you**

> And Moses stretched out his hand over the sea; and the Lord caused the sea to go back by a strong east wind all that night, and made the sea dry land, and the waters were divided.[215]

92 caused manna to descend upon you

> And the Lord spake unto Moses, saying, I have heard the murmurings of the children of Israel: speak unto them, saying, At even ye shall eat flesh, and in the morning ye shall be filled with bread: and ye shall know that I am the Lord your God. And it came to pass, that at even the quails came up, and covered the camp: and in the morning the dew lay round the host. And when the dew that lay was gone up, behold, upon the face of the wilderness there lay a small round thing, as small as the hoar frost on the ground. And when the children of Israel saw it, they said one to another, It is manna: for they wist not what it was, And Moses said unto them, This is the bread which the Lord hath given you to eat.[216]

See also notes at 5 and 22 regarding **bread**.

92 the cloud to overshadow you

> And the Lord said unto Moses, Lo, I come unto thee in a thick cloud that the people may hear when I speak with thee, and believe thee for ever. And Moses told the words of the people unto the Lord . . . And it came to pass on the third day in the morning, that there were thunders and lightnings, and a thick cloud upon the mount, and the voice of the trumpet exceeding loud; so that all the people that was in the camp trembled.[217]

> And he reared up the court round the tabernacle and the altar, and set up the hanging of the court gate. So Moses finished the work.
> Then a cloud covered the tent of the congregation, and the glory of the Lord filled the tabernacle. And when the cloud was taken up from over the tabernacle, the children of Israel went onward in all their journeys: But if the cloud were not taken up, then they journeyed not till the day that it was taken up. For the cloud of the Lord was upon the tabernacle

by day. and fire was on it by night, in the sight of all
the house of Israel, throughout all their journeys.[218]

92 **Who delivered you from Pharaoh**

> And I will dwell among the children of Israel, and will
> be their God. And they shall know that I am the Lord
> their God, that brought them forth out of the land of
> Egypt, that I may dwell among them: I am the Lord
> their God.[219]

See Exodus for the entire account of the deliverance
of the Israelites.

92 **exalted you above all human beings** Reference to the
Jews as the chosen people of God as in Exodus:

> And the Lord said . . . Come now therefore, and I will
> send thee unto Pharaoh, that thou mayest bring my
> people the children of Israel out of Egypt.[220]

92 **Nebuchadnezzar** King of Babylon who in 599 BC
captured Jerusalem. In 588 he destroyed the holy city
and removed most of the inhabitants to Chaldaea.

92 **Amalekites** Expelled in early times from Babylonia,
they spread through Arabia to Palestine, Syria and
Egypt. They were bitter opponents of Israel and
suffered a crushing defeat from Saul.

92 **Pentateuch** The Greek name given to the first five
books of the Old Testament which are commonly
ascribed to Moses and known also as the Torah.

93 **Mecca and Medina** Two sacred cities in the Arabian
province of Ḥijáz, the Holy Land of the Muslims.
Mecca was the birthplace of Muḥammad and is the site
of Islám's most sacred shrine, the Ka'bih. Medina is

the settlement that gave refuge to the Prophet and became His burial-place; to a Muslim it is second in sanctity only to Mecca. See also **Baṭḥá unto Yathrib** at 54 above.

93 **verses of the Pentateuch, that referred to His Manifestation** Note, for example, the following passage on the coming of the Manifestations:

> And he said, The Lord came from Sinai, and rose up from Seir unto them; he shined forth from mount Paran, and he came with ten thousands of saints: from his right hand went a fiery law for them.[221]

94 **'. . . and then, after they had understood it, distorted it, and knew that they did so.'** Compare this with 'Abdu'l-Bahá's comment about Covenant-breakers:

> These do not doubt the validity of the Covenant but selfish motives have dragged them to this condition. It is not that they do not know what they do – they are perfectly aware and still they exhibit opposition.[222]

97 **untutored holy Men** Consider Bahá'u'lláh's description of this lack of education:

> We ask thee to reflect upon that which hath been revealed, and to be fair and just in thy speech, that perchance the splendours of the day-star or truthfulness and sincerity may shine forth . . . This Wronged One hath frequented no school, neither hath He attended the controversies of the learned. By My life! Not of Mine own volition have I revealed Myself, but God, of His own choosing, hath manifested Me.[223]

> We have not entered any school, nor read any of your dissertations. Incline your ears to the words of this unlettered One, wherewith He summoneth you unto God, the Ever-Abiding.[224]

98 Jesus had disappeared . . . and ascended

> Verily the heaven into which the Messiah rose up was not this unending sky, rather was His heaven the Kingdom of His beneficent Lord. Even as He Himself hath said, 'I came down from heaven', and again, 'The Son of Man is in heaven.' Hence it is clear that His heaven is beyond all directional points; it encircleth all existence, and is raised up for those who worship God. Beg and implore thy Lord to lift thee up into that heaven, and give thee to eat of its food, in this age of majesty and might.[225]

98 fourth heaven

> As to the ascent of Christ to the 'fourth heaven' as revealed in the glorious Book of Íqán, he [the Guardian] stated that the 'fourth heaven' is a term used and a belief held by the early astronomers. The followers of the Shí'ih sect likewise held this belief. As the Kitáb-i-Íqán was revealed for the guidance of that sect, this term was used in conformity with the concepts of its followers.[226]

In the ancient scheme of the seven heavens or spheres, the sun was located in the fourth heaven. See also Íqán, para. 144.

99 Morn is breaking Allusion to Bahá'u'lláh's own Revelation.

99 'Verily, we are God's . . . and unto Him we do return.' Qur'án 2:156. See also Íqán, para. 279.

99 eye of thine heart Throughout the Bahá'í writings reference is made to two ways of seeing, to the 'inner and outer eyes'. This inner vision, or inspired insight, associated with 'the eye of thine heart', must be cleansed of earthly things and directed towards that

true knowledge shining from the Word of God, the light of the True One. Consider the following well-known admonition:

> O Man of Two Visions! Close one eye and open the other. Close one to the world and all that is therein, and open the other to the hallowed beauty of the Beloved.[227]

100 **O affectionate seeker!** This paragraph sets out three distinct degrees of divine recognition characterized as 'the holy realm of the spirit' in which the soul, beholding naught but God, is free from need for lesser testimonies; 'the sacred domain of truth' where the knowledge of all things depends on His recognition; and finally 'the land of testimony' where the seeker contents himself with the proof of the Book. In a sense, these three perspectives may be said to parallel the three stages of certitude alluded to by Bahá'u'lláh. See note on the **stations of absolute certitude** at 216 below.

100 **'God was alone . . .'** Tradition attributed to the Imám 'Alí and others.

100 **'This proof is His Word . . .'** Tradition attributed to the Imám 'Alí.

101 **people of the Bayán** The followers of the Báb, known also as Bábís. Bahá'u'lláh later exhorted and admonished the followers of the Báb in numerous passages. To cite but one instance:

> O people of the Bayán! We have chosen you out of the world to know and recognize Our Self. We have caused you to draw nigh unto the right side of Paradise – the Spot out of which the undying Fire crieth

in manifold accents: 'There is none other God besides Me, the All-Powerful, the Most High!' Take
heed lest ye allow yourselves to be shut out as by a
veil from this Day Star that shineth above the day-
spring of the Will of your Lord, the All-Merciful, and
whose light hath encompassed both the small and the
great. Purge your sight, that ye may perceive its glory
with your own eyes, and depend not on the sight of
any one except your self, for God hath never bur-
dened any soul beyond its power. Thus hath it been
sent down unto the Prophets and Messengers of old,
and been recorded in all the Scriptures.[228]

Eventually the majority of the Bábís recognized
Bahá'u'lláh as the Promised One announced by the
Báb. For **Bayán** see notes at 1 above and 219 below.

101 **the King of divine might** Shoghi Effendi cites this
sentence in his exposition of the inconceivable greatness of Bahá'u'lláh's Revelation in *God Passes By*, pp.
98–9 and states clearly that Bahá'u'lláh is alluding
here to Himself. In the light of this clarification re-
read the titles in the preceding lines: 'He, Who is the
Quintessence of truth, the inmost Reality of all things,
the Source of all light.'

Part Two

The second part of the text centres on the sovereignty of
the Manifestations of God and their mysterious two-fold
nature. It also unravels the inner meaning of numerous
abstruse scriptural terms and, finally, demonstrates the
validity of the Mission of the Báb and His Revelation.

103 **sent down from their invisible habitations** 'The
Prophets, unlike us, are pre-existent. The soul of
Christ existed in the spiritual world before His birth

in this world. We cannot imagine what that world is like, so words are inadequate to picture His state of being.'[229]

103 **this world** This realm of creation is one of three worlds of existence described in the Bahá'í writings: the World of God, which is infinite, limitless and perfect; the world of the Kingdom of Command, which is the Holy Reality of the Manifestations of God, the Primal Will; and the world of existence or servitude, which includes the many worlds of creation both visible and invisible. See *Some Answered Questions*, p. 295. These three conditions of existence are represented in the Bahá'í ringstone symbol by the three parallel lines.

103 **educate the souls of men and endue with grace** Bahá'u'lláh, likewise, states:

> God's purpose in sending His Prophets unto men is twofold. The first is to liberate the children of men from the darkness of ignorance, and guide them to the light of true understanding. The second is to ensure the peace and tranquillity of mankind, and provide all the means by which they can be established.[230]

103 **'Verily God doeth . . .'** See also *Gleanings from the Writings of Bahá'u'lláh*, pp. 206, 209, 284, 295; Íqán paras. 155, 182, 184; *Proclamation of Bahá'u'lláh*, p. 13; *Kitáb-i-Aqdas*, paras. 7, 47, 157. The phrase itself is a composite of two Qur'ánic verses, 14:27 and 5:2.

104 **Far be it from His glory that human tongue . . . recount His praise**

Every praise which any tongue or pen can recount,

every imagination which any heart can devise, is debarred from the station which Thy most exalted Pen hath ordained, how much more must it fall short of the heights which Thou hast Thyself immensely exalted above the conception and the description of any creature. For the attempt of the evanescent to conceive the signs of the Uncreated is as the stirring of the drop before the tumult of Thy billowing oceans.[231]

I render Thee thanks, O Thou Who hast lighted Thy fire within my soul, and cast the beams of Thy light into my heart, that Thou hast taught Thy servants how to make mention of Thee, and revealed unto them the ways whereby they can supplicate Thee, through Thy most holy and exalted tongue, and Thy most august and precious speech. But for Thy leave, who is there that could venture to express Thy might and Thy grandeur; and were it not for Thine instruction, who is the man that could discover the ways of Thy pleasure in the kingdom of Thy creation?[232]

104 **everlastingly hidden**   'From time immemorial He hath been veiled in the ineffable sanctity of His exalted Self, and will everlastingly continue to be wrapt in the impenetrable mystery of His unknowable Essence.'[233]

104 **No tie of direct intercourse**

He is, and hath from everlasting been, one and alone, without peer or equal, eternal in the past, eternal in the future, detached from all things, ever-abiding, unchangeable, and self-subsisting. He hath assigned no associate unto Himself in His Kingdom, no counsellor to counsel Him, none to compare unto Him, none to rival His glory.[234]

104 **Primal Will**   This theme is found in numerous passages of the Bahá'í writings. One instance is the following extract from the writings of the Báb:

. . . know thou that the First Remembrance, which is the Primal Will of God, may be likened unto the sun. God hath created Him through the potency of His might, and He hath, from the beginning that hath no beginning, caused Him to be manifested in every Dispensation through the compelling power of His behest, and God will, to the end that knoweth no end, continue to manifest Him according to the good-pleasure of His invincible Purpose . . . It is this Primal Will which appeareth resplendent in every Prophet and speaketh forth in every revealed Book . . .

In the time of the First Manifestation the Primal Will appeared in Adam; in the day of Noah It became known in Noah; in the day of Abraham in Him; and so in the day of Moses; the day of Jesus; the day of Muḥammad, the Apostle of God; the day of the 'Point of the Bayán'; the day of Him Whom God shall make manifest; and the day of the One Who will appear after Him Whom God shall make manifest. Hence the inner meaning of the words uttered by the Apostle of God, 'I am all the Prophets', inasmuch as what shineth resplendent in each one of Them hath been and will ever remain the one and the same sun.[235]

105 **God would have you beware of Himself** Beyond the obvious meaning of this verse, the term 'Himself' has been understood by some scholars to refer to the Manifestation of God. This seems to conform to Bahá'u'lláh's use of the expression 'Self of God' at times to refer to Himself and the other Prophets. This, however, should be viewed in the light of the explanation given in the following paragraph of the text itself, especially the closing lines.

105 **'God was alone . . .'** A tradition attributed to Imám 'Alí and others. In the face of God, all else is obliterated and as nothing.

105 **their inability**

> All the Embodiments of His Names wander in the
> wilderness of search, athirst and eager to discover His
> Essence, and all the Manifestations of His Attributes
> implore Him, from the Sinai of Holiness, to unravel
> His mystery . . . Ten thousand Prophets, each a
> Moses, are thunderstruck upon the Sinai of their
> search at His forbidding voice, 'Thou shalt never
> behold Me!'; whilst a myriad Messengers, each as
> great as Jesus, stand dismayed upon their heavenly
> thrones by the interdiction, 'Mine Essence thou shalt
> never apprehend!' [236]

106 **'His grace hath transcended all things . . .'** The first
half of this verse is by Bahá'u'lláh; the second half is
Qur'ánic in origin.

106 **Exponents on earth of Him Who is the central Orb
of the universe**

> We find God only through the Intermediary of His
> Prophet. We see the Perfection of God in His Proph-
> ets. Time and space are physical things; God, the
> Creator, is not a 'place' as we conceive of place in
> physical terms. God is the Infinite Essence, the
> Creator. We cannot picture Him or His state, but if
> we did, we would be His equals, not His creatures.
> God is never flesh, but mirrored in the attributes of
> His Prophets we see His Divine characteristics and
> perfections. [237]

106 **'There is no distinction . . .'** Tradition attributed to
the Imám Mihdí, the twelfth Imám.

106 **'I am He, Himself . . .'** Ḥadíth-i-Qudsí of
Muḥammad. Compare with the following alternative
rendering: 'Manifold are Our relationships with God.
At one time, We are He Himself, and He is We

Ourself. At another He is that He is, and We are that We are.'[238]

107 **'Man is My Mystery . . .'** Ḥadíth-i-Qudsí of Muḥammad.

107 **the eternal King** Reference to the Imám 'Alí, who is the author of the tradition which immediately follows.

107 **'He hath known God who hath known himself'** Bahá'u'lláh has elaborated on the meaning of this tradition, attributed to the Imám 'Alí, in a Tablet addressed to Mírzá Hádíy-i-Qazvíní, one of the Letters of the Living. In this Tablet He reveals that this saying has unique and wondrous meanings in all of the worlds of God in accordance with the exigencies of each world. No one who has failed to attain these worlds can grasp such meanings. If all the oceans were converted to ink and all the pens on earth set to writing it would not suffice to mention all these meanings. He then offers a dewdrop from this infinite ocean for the guidance of seekers. A significant portion of the explanation which follows constitutes section LXXXIII, pp. 164–6 of *Gleanings from the Writings of Bahá'u'lláh*, which begins: 'Consider the rational faculty . . .' See also ibid. p. 326.

109 **'Hath aught else save Thee a power . . .'** Imám Ḥusayn, in the Prayer of the Day of 'Arafah.

109 **eternal King** Reference to the Imám 'Alí.

109 **'No thing have I perceived . . .'** Words of Imám 'Alí.

109 **tradition of Kumayl** By this tradition is meant one of the traditions which Kumayl Ibn Ziyád Nakha'í has related on the authority of the Imám 'Alí; quoted in

the Bihár (see note under 272 below). Kumayl was a devoted apostle of 'Alí who attained the crown of martyrdom through his love for him.

113 **Qá'im** The Promised One of the <u>Sh</u>í'ís. See note at 90 above.

113 **sovereignty of the Qá'im**

> Bahá'u'lláh, Who Himself was an active figure in those days and was regarded one of the leading exponents of the Faith of the Báb, states clearly His views in the Íqán that His conception of the sovereignty of the Promised Qá'im was purely a spiritual one, and not a material or political one . . .[239]

114 **'Abdu'lláh-i-Ubayy** Opponent of Muḥammad; a pagan divine who was chief of the hypocrites. The Muslim commentators relate that he was a tall man of a very graceful presence and of a ready and eloquent tongue. He used to frequent the Prophet's assembly, attended by several like himself. These men were greatly admired by Muḥammad, who was taken with their handsome appearance and listened to their discourse with pleasure. 'Abdu'lláh-i-Ubayy was said to have kept six slave girls for prostitution; one of them complained to Muḥammad and in response Qur'án 24:33 was revealed: 'Force not your female slaves into sin, in order that ye may gain the casual fruitions of this world, if they wish to preserve their modesty.' He promised help to the Jewish Baní Naḍír if they stayed in Medina and fought the Prophet following their violation of the covenant they made with Him. He drew off 300 men from battle by predicting their certain death in the expedition of Tabúr. In his last sickness (he died in the ninth year of the Hijra), his son came and asked Muḥammad to beg

pardon of God for his father, which the Prophet did. 'Abdu'lláh-i-Ubayy then asked to see Muḥammad and to be buried in His shirt. Verses of the Qur'án indicate, however, that in general the hypocrites will not be forgiven. See Súrih 63.

114 **Abú-'Ámir, the hermit** Known as ar-Ráhib, the Hermit, because of earlier ascetic practices. A Medinian renegade who strongly opposed Muḥammad. After being put to flight in the battle of Ḥunayn, he fled to Syria in hopes of raising an army with help from the Byzantine emperor but died there, in Kinnisrín. He was to have dedicated a hypocrites' mosque at Qubá', in the immediate vicinity of Medina, the construction of which he is said to have inspired. See Qur'án 9:107.

114 **Ka'b-Ibn-i-Ashraf** Medinian half-Jewish priest, poet and inveterate enemy of Muḥammad. After the Prophet suffered a temporary defeat, he broke agreements with Him and went to Mecca with 40 horsemen. There he conspired with Muḥammad's arch-enemy Abú Sufyán in an alliance to bring about the Prophet's death. As a consequence he was slain and the Prophet ordered his followers, the Baní Naḍír, to leave Medina. See Qur'án 59:2.

114 **Naḍr-Ibn-i-Ḥárith** One of 'nine persons who made mischief in the land'.[240] Also referred to at 33:6; because, it is said, he brought from Persia the romance of Rustam and Isfandiyar and recited it in the assemblies of the Quraysh. Reported to have challenged God thus: 'O God, if what Muḥammad preaches be the truth from Thee, rain down upon us a shower of stones, or send some dreadful judgement to punish us.' See Qur'án 70:1.

115 **'No Prophet of God hath suffered . . .'** Ḥadíth of Muḥammad.

116 **Gabriel** The angel-mediator of revelation to Muḥammad. See note at 54 above.

118 **one single verse** The identification of the well-known verse referred to is not clearly given. Consider, nevertheless, how a Qur'ánic verse such as 'Verily, I am the Messenger of God unto you all' (7:18) uttered by Muḥammad would produce the results mentioned. Acceptance or denial of the truth of this one verse would suffice.

118 **the Satan of self** 'Abdu'l-Bahá, when asked, 'What is Satan?' replied, 'The insistent self.'[241] In the Bahá'í teachings Satan is not viewed as an independent force but rather as the natural inclinations of man's lower nature, his animal nature. This lower nature, symbolized as Satan, is the ego inclined to evil which is a part of each human soul. It is not an outside personality:

> God has never created an evil spirit; all such ideas and nomenclature are symbols expressing the mere human or earthly nature of man. It is an essential condition of the soil of earth that thorns, weeds and fruitless trees may grow from it. Relatively speaking, this is evil; it is simply the lower state and baser product of nature.[242]

118 **Kawthar** A river in paradise. See note at 25 above.

120 **'Swift is He in reckoning.'** Qur'án 2:202; 3:19, 199; 5:4; 13:41; 14:51; 24:39; 40:17.

122 **Seraph of God** Here, literally, Isráfíl, the angel of the Judgement Day who, according to Islám, calls the dead to rise to new life.

As by the will of God the power of composition exists, so, also by will of God the power of decomposition exists.

These two are expressed in scripture by 'Isráfíl' the angel who gives life to men, and the Angel of Death who takes it away. The first is the power of composition or attraction, the other the power of decomposition. They are not angels.[243]

123 **by 'resurrection' is meant**

. . . Concerning the meaning of 'Resurrection': although this term is often used by Bahá'u'lláh in His Writings, as in the passage quoted in your letter, its meaning is figurative. The tomb mentioned is also allegorical, i.e. the tomb of unbelief. The Day of Resurrection, according to Bahá'í interpretation, is the Judgement Day, the Day when unbelievers will be called upon to give account of their actions, and whether the world has prevented them from acknowledging the new Revelation.[244]

123 **'paradise' and 'hell'** The symbolic meaning of these terms revolves around the acceptance and denial of the Manifestation of God. Bahá'u'lláh reveals:

They say: 'Where is Paradise, and where is Hell?' Say: 'The one is reunion with Me; the other thine own self, O thou who dost associate a partner with God and doubtest.'[245]

In this regard the Báb wrote:

There is no paradise, in the estimation of the believers in the Divine Unity, more exalted than to obey God's commandments, and there is no fire in the eyes of those who have known God and His signs, fiercer than to transgress His laws and to oppress another soul, even to the extent of a mustard seed.[246]

Relative to the Paradise explained by Muḥammad in the Qur'án, such utterances are spiritual and are cast into the mould of words and figures of speech; for at that time people did not possess the capacity of comprehending spiritual significances.[247]

125 born of the Spirit

I render Thee thanks, therefore, and extol Thee, in the name of all them that are dear to Thee, for that Thou hast caused them to be born again, by reason of the living waters which have flowed down out of the mouth of Thy will.[248]

127 **Kúfih**   An erstwhile city on the west bank of the Euphrates, south of Karbilá, where the Imám 'Alí established the seat of his Imamate. Most of its early inhabitants were unfaithful to the Imáms. It was an important Muslim seat of learning which later disappeared entirely.

127 **'Alí, the Commander of the Faithful**   The illustrious first Imám and rightful successor of Muḥammad. He was a cousin of the Prophet and husband of His daughter Fáṭimih. He was killed at Kúfih by Ibn-i-Muljam in 661 AD. See note on **immaculate Souls** at 33 above.

127 **Ṣiráṭ**   'The Bridge' which Muslim tradition holds will be extended over Hell on the Last Days over which men will have to cross to attain Paradise.

Take ye good heed that ye may all, under the leadership of Him Who is the Source of Divine Guidance, be enabled to direct your steps aright upon the Bridge, which is sharper than the sword and finer than a hair, so that perchance the things which from the beginning of thy life till the end thou hast performed for the love of God, may not, all at once and unrealized by thyself, be turned to acts not acceptable in the sight of God.[249]

128 **true believer liveth** Bahá'u'lláh has explained
the meaning of this saying of Muḥammad in a
Tablet revealed after the Íqán, affirming that its
truth is manifest as the sun. After stating that the
existence and life of the true believer are to be
regarded as 'the originating purpose of all creation', He explains that 'the true believer' will
'eternally live and endure. His spirit will everlastingly circle round the Will of God. He will last as
long as God, Himself, will last.'[250]

129 **Ḥamzih** 'Abdu'l-Muṭṭalib, 'Prince of Martyrs',
Muḥammad's uncle. Slain at the battle of Uḥud
by Waḥshí; the infidels abused his dead body by
removing the bowels and cutting off his nose and
ears. When Muḥammad saw it, He swore to retali-
ate but God revealed verses to Him to abstain and
voided thus His oath. See Súrih 16. Muḥammad
later forgave Waḥshí.

129 **Abú-Jahl** Muslim epithet meaning 'Father of
Ignorance'; refers to 'Amr Ibn Hishám, entitled
Abú'l-Ḥakím, 'Father of Wisdom'. One of the
prominent Meccans who opposed Muḥammad;
slain in the battle of Badr; condemned to 'eternal
damnation'. He once threatened that if he caught
Muḥammad in the act of adoration, he would set
his foot on His neck; but when he came upon Him
in that posture, he suddenly turned back as in a
fright, and, being asked what was the matter, said
there was a ditch of fire between himself and
Muḥammad and he had seen a vision of terrible
troops come to defend Him.[251]

129 **Kawthar** A river in paradise. See note at 25 above.

131 **the potency of one word**   Bahá'u'lláh, in a prayer, elaborates on the power of a single word:

> I testify that if Thy servants were to turn towards Thee with the eyes Thou didst create in them and with the ears wherewith Thou didst endow them, they would all be carried away by a single word sent down from the right hand of the throne of Thy majesty. That word alone would suffice to brighten their faces, and to assure their hearts, and to cause their souls to soar up to the atmosphere of Thy great glory, and to ascend into the heaven of Thy sovereignty.[252]

> Those souls who have the capacity and ability to receive the outpourings of the Kingdom and the confirmation of the Holy Spirit, they become attracted through one word . . . No sooner is the oil touched by fire than it is ignited . . .[253]

See also Íqán, para. 101.

134 **'He is the Dominant, above all things.'**   Bahá'u'lláh's own words.

135 **Ḥusayn**   The third Imám; son of 'Alí and Fáṭimih; the 'Prince of Martyrs', tragically slain at Karbilá. See note at 138 below for details. Ḥusayn's exalted position and Bahá'u'lláh's identifying Himself with his return are explained:

> Imám Ḥusayn has, as attested by the Íqán, been endowed with special grace and power among the Imáms, hence the mystical reference to Bahá'u'lláh as the return of Imám Ḥusayn, meaning the Revelation in Bahá'u'lláh of those attributes with which Imám Ḥusayn had been specifically endowed.[254]

> In the prayer[255] . . . Bahá'u'lláh identifies Himself with Imám Ḥusayn. This does not make him a

Prophet, but his position was very unique, and we know Bahá'u'lláh claims to be the 'return' of the Imám Ḥusayn. He, in other words, identifies His Spirit with these Holy Souls gone before, that does not, of course, make Him in any way their reincarnation. Nor does it mean all of them were Prophets.[256]

See also Íqán, paras. 138, 139, 179, 251.

135 **'There was none to equal or to match him . . .'** Bahá'u'lláh's own words.

136 **Karbilá** Site of the martyrdom and shrine of the Imám Ḥusayn and consequently a holy city for the Shí'ís; located some 88 kilometres (55 miles) southwest of Baghdád on the Euphrates River.

136 **land of Ṭaff** Another name for Karbilá and its surrounding plain.

138 **circumstances that have attended the martyrdom of Ḥusayn** Ḥusayn, the third Imám, died in an historic episode which has had tremendous repercussions on the Shí'ís through the centuries. He and a band of his family and supporters, numbering 72 according to the accounts, were surrounded by an immense force representing the Umayyad Caliph, Yazíd. This host of thousands of men intercepted Ḥusayn near Karbilá as he travelled north on his way to asylum in Kúfa in 680 AD. The Umayyads were demanding his pledge of allegiance in denial of his right of succession as the head of Islám:

> The fighting appears to have been of a sporadic nature consisting of single combat and brief forays. The steady fire maintained by the Umayyad archers on Husayn's camp took its own toll. One by one Husayn's supporters fell and then the members of his

family until only he and his half-brother 'Abbás, the standard-bearer on that day, were left of the fighting men. 'Abbás was killed trying to obtain water for the thirsty women and children and the army converged on the lone figure of Husayn.

Carrying his infant son in his arms, Husayn pleaded for water for the babe but an arrow lodged in the baby's throat killing him. As the troops closed around him, Husayn fought valiantly until at last he was struck a severe blow that caused him to fall face down on the ground. Even then the soldiers hesitated to deal the final blow to the grandson of the Prophet until Shimr ordered them on, and according to some accounts himself came forward and struck the blow that ended Husayn's life.

The Umayyad army looted the tents, decapitated the bodies of all Husayn's companions and raised these on spears to lead their procession back to Kúfa. The women and children who had been taken prisoner included 'Alí, the only surviving son of Husayn, who had been too ill to participate in the fighting.

At Kúfa 'Ubaydu'lláh convened a great assembly and ordered the head of Husayn to be brought to him on a tray and also the captives. When the head was placed before him, 'Ubaydu'lláh struck the lips with his cane and taunted the captives. Some of those witnessing this scene were intensely moved and one of them spoke up saying: 'Remove your cane from those lips, for, by God, many a time have I seen the lips of the Prophet of God on those lips.'[257]

140 **the mysteries of Ḥusayn's martyrdom** At a later stage in His ministry Bahá'u'lláh revealed a lengthy and detailed Tablet of Visitation for the Imám Ḥusayn in which He refers to His martyrdom as the most great calamity and as a grievous affliction. Through Ḥusayn's martyrdom the soul of the Chaste One (Fáṭimih) was melted and the Apostle (Muḥammad) lamented, the inmates of the supreme paradise cried out and the realities of existence were consumed.

Bahá'u'lláh refers to Ḥusayn as the Prince and King of Martyrs, the Pride and Beloved of Martyrs. Through him the light of detachment shone forth in the world and the near ones were adorned with the ornament of piety. If it were not for Ḥusayn the injunction of the 'B' and the 'E' would not have been manifested, the choice Wine would not have been unsealed, the Bird of divine testimony would not have sung forth, and the Tongue of Grandeur would not have spoken amongst the followers of divers beliefs. By him, Bahá'u'lláh states, the mystery of true knowledge became manifest in every land and the light of certitude shone forth from the heaven of testimony. Through him the doors of divine grace were unlocked to the world. For nine pages Bahá'u'lláh continues to extol the wonders and effects of Ḥusayn and his great sacrifice.[258]

144 **Pilate** A pagan Roman procurator of Judaea at the time of Christ's crucifixion, 26–36 AD, who issued His death-sentence.[259] 'Surviving records of Pilate's governorship, and especially those from Jewish sources, picture him as greedy and bloodthirsty. Josephus, for example, implies that his career in Judaea was splashed with gore from beginning to end.'[260] ' . . . in the year 36, after quieting an outburst in Samaria with unnecessary ruthlessness, he was sent by the legate of Syria, the ranking official in the near East, to Rome to defend his misdeeds. Of his end nothing is known.'[261] A fourth century tradition states that in 39 AD, at the order of the Emperor Caligula, Pilate killed himself.

144 **Caiaphas** Joseph Caiaphas, the 'leading divine of that age', having been appointed to the Jewish high priesthood not earlier than 18 AD by Roman authority. Powerful and unscrupulous, he was suspected by most Jews of collusion with his Roman masters. He presided

at the court which condemned Jesus Christ. As Bahá'u-'lláh later revealed:

> . . . call thou to mind the one who sentenced Jesus to death. He was the most learned of his age in his own country, whilst he who was only a fisherman believed in Him. Take good heed and be of them that observe the warning.[262]

See John 18:14.

144 **'Didst thou not claim to be the Divine Messiah?'** See Matthew 26:62–5.

144 **fourth heaven** See note at 98 above.

146 **Point of the Bayán** Reference to the Báb, the Revealer of the Bayán. Bahá'u'lláh subsequently affirmed with regard to Himself: 'He around Whom the Point of the Bayán (Báb) hath revolved is come.'[263] For **Bayán** see note at 1 above and 219 below.

148 **contention, that all Revelation is ended** Bahá'u'lláh states in the Súriy-i-Ṣabr:

> God hath sent down His Messengers to succeed to Moses and Jesus, and He will continue to do so till 'the end that hath no end'; so that His grace may, from the heaven of Divine bounty, be continually vouchsafed to mankind.[264]

The Bahá'í teachings thus clearly affirm the coming of future Manifestations of God and repudiate any claim to finality for the Messages of the Báb and Bahá'u'lláh.

> Indeed, the categorical rejection by the followers of the Faith of Bahá'u'lláh of the claim to finality which

any religious system inaugurated by the Prophets of the past may advance is as clear and emphatic as their own refusal to claim that same finality for the Revelation with which they stand identified. 'To believe that all revelation is ended, that the portals of Divine mercy are closed, that from the daysprings of eternal holiness no sun shall rise again, that the ocean of everlasting bounty is forever stilled, and that out of the tabernacle of ancient glory the Messengers of God have ceased to be made manifest' must constitute in the eyes of every follower of the Faith a grave, an inexcusable departure from one of its most cherished and fundamental principles.[265]

Note how Shoghi Effendi has reinforced his argument in this passage by citing the very words of the Íqán being commented on here.

148 Presence of God

In all the Divine Books the promise of the Divine Presence hath been explicitly recorded. By this Presence is meant the Presence of Him Who is the Dayspring of the signs, and the Dawning-Place of the clear tokens, and the Manifestation of the Excellent Names, and the Source of the attributes, of the true God, exalted be His glory. God in His Essence and in His own Self hath ever been unseen, inaccessible, and unknowable. By Presence, therefore, is meant the Presence of the One Who is His Viceregent amongst men. He, moreover, hath never had, nor hath He, any peer or likeness. For were He to have any peer or likeness, how could it then be demonstrated that His being is exalted above, and His essence sanctified from, all comparison and likeness? Briefly, there hath been revealed in the Kitáb-i-Íqán (Book of Certitude) concerning the Presence and Revelation of God that which will suffice the fair-minded.[266]

149 Universal Revelation For notes on this and the other

two stages of Divine Revelation, see section 7, 'The Three Stages of Divine Revelation'. Consider also the following explanation of Bahá'u'lláh with regard to the general or universal Revelation which exists in all things:

> Know thou that every created thing is a sign of the revelation of God. Each, according to its capacity, is, and will ever remain, a token of the Almighty. Inasmuch as He, the sovereign Lord of all, hath willed to reveal His sovereignty in the kingdom of names and attributes, each and every created thing hath, through the act of the Divine Will, been made a sign of His glory. So pervasive and general is this revelation that nothing whatsoever in the whole universe can be discovered that doth not reflect His splendour. Under such conditions every consideration of proximity and remoteness is obliterated . . . Were the Hand of Divine power to divest of this high endowment all created things, the entire universe would become desolate and void.[267]

150 **Most Holy Outpouring . . . Holy Outpouring** These terms are mentioned in the works of a number of Muslim Ṣúfí writers such as Ibn'ul-'Arabí, Rúmí and Jámí. The 'Most Holy Outpouring' is said to refer to the manifestation of God unto Himself. In this state every attribute of God is the same as God Himself. He is the essence of love, of knowledge, etc. He is Himself love. The 'Holy Outpouring' refers here to the effulgences of God witnessed in the Manifestations of God.

150 **'The way is barred . . .'** Tradition attributed to the Imám 'Alí.

151 **'Presence of God'** See Bahá'u'lláh's Tablet of Visitation: '. . . he who hath attained unto Thy presence hath attained unto the presence of God.'[268]

152 **'When the Qá'im riseth . . .'** Tradition attributed to the Imám Ṣádiq.

155 **'The abased amongst you, He shall exalt . . .'** Tradition of the Imám 'Alí, in the Nahju'l-Baláh<u>gh</u>í. Bahá'u'lláh, in one of His Tablets, cites an example of this spiritual phenomenon from the history of Islám. He states that when Muḥammad appeared,

> . . . the learned men of Mecca and Medina arose, in the early days of His Revelation, against Him and rejected His Message, while they who were destitute of all learning recognized and embraced His Faith. Ponder a while. Consider how Balál, the Ethiopian, unlettered though he was, ascended into the heaven of faith and certitude, whilst 'Abdu'lláh Ubayy, a leader among the learned, maliciously strove to oppose Him. Behold, how a mere shepherd was so carried away by the ecstasy of the words of God that he was able to gain admittance into the habitation of his Best-Beloved, and was united to Him Who is the Lord of Mankind, whilst they who prided themselves on their knowledge and wisdom strayed far from His path and remained deprived of His grace. For this reason He hath written: 'He that is exalted among you shall be abased, and he that is abased shall be exalted.' References to this theme are to be found in most of the heavenly Books, as well as in the sayings of the Prophets and Messengers of God.[269]

Bahá'u'lláh refers to Balál, mentioned above, with regard to his mispronunciation of the Arabic letter '<u>sh</u>ín', asserting, 'The acts of his honour, Balál, the Ethiopian, were so acceptable in the sight of God that the "sín" of his stuttering tongue excelled the "<u>sh</u>ín" pronounced by all the world.'[270]

155 **'To seek evidence . . .'** Saying of the 'ulamá.

155 **Behold this flamelike-Youth . . . in the land** Clear reference to Bahá'u'lláh and His prophetic mission.

155 **'Iráq** Part of the Turkish Ottoman Empire in 1862 when the Íqán was revealed. Now an independent Arab nation with its capital at Baghdád.

157 **a sacrifice which fire out of heaven shall devour** This was considered by the Jews to be one of the signs which all of the Prophets were to produce. Through prayer these Messengers could call down fire from on high to consume the sacrifice. The same then was demanded of Muḥammad. 'Abdu'l-Bahá is said to have unfolded the spiritual significance of such burnt offerings, interpreting the altar as the heart, the ewes and lambs as man's lower passions and desires, and the fire from heaven as the fire of the love of God which consumes the offering and thus cleanses the heart.

157 **Abel and Cain** The occasion of Abel and Cain making the sacrificial offering is related according to Muslim tradition thus: Each of them was born with a twin sister. When they were grown up, Adam, following God's direction, ordered Cain to marry Abel's twin sister and Abel to marry Cain's. This Cain refused to do because his own sister was the more comely. Adam then commanded them to make their offerings to God, thereby referring the dispute to His determination. Cain's offering was a sheaf of the very worst of his corn; Abel's a fat lamb, of the best of his flock. God declared His acceptance of Abel's sacrifice in a visible manner, by causing fire to descend from heaven and consume it, leaving Cain's offering untouched. Abel was the stronger of the two and could easily have prevailed against his brother, but he let Cain slay him for he would not stretch forth his hand against him.[271]

159 **'He of Whom they had knowledge'**

> Various Traditions cited in Aṭ-Ṭabarí's 'Jámi'u'l-Bayán' support this understanding, as, for instance, the following from Mujáhid: '[The Jews] would implore the assistance of [the expected] Muḥammad, saying that He would appear; "yet when there came unto them that of which they had knowledge", and he was not of them [the Jews], "they disbelieved in Him"'; or the following, from Sa'íd Ibn Jubayr: '"Yet when there came to them that of which they had knowledge, they disbelieved in Him"; those intended are the Jews: they recognized Muḥammad as a Prophet, yet disbelieved in Him.'[272]

160 **return** For a further explanation by Bahá'u'lláh of the meanings of 'return' see Súriy-i-Vafá, in *Tablets of Bahá'u'lláh Revealed after the Kitáb-i-Aqdas*, pp. 183–7.

161 **regarded as one soul and the same person**

> The Prophets 'regarded as One and the same person' include the Lesser Prophets as well, and not merely Those Who bring a 'Book'. The station is different, but they are Prophets and Their nature thus different from that of ours.[273]

See also Íqán, paras. 19, 192–3.

161 **Kawthar** A river in Paradise. See note at 25 above.

161 **'I am all the Prophets.'** Consider the following passage from a Tablet of Bahá'u'lláh in a similar light:

> O Jews! If ye be intent on crucifying once again Jesus, the Spirit of God, put Me to death, for He hath once more, in My person, been made manifest unto you. Deal with Me as ye wish, for I have vowed to lay down My life in the path of God. I will fear no one, though

the powers of earth and heaven be leagued against Me. Followers of the Gospel! If ye cherish the desire to slay Muḥammad, the Apostle of God, seize Me and put an end to My life, for I am He, and My Self is His Self. Do unto Me as ye like, for the deepest longing of Mine heart is to attain the presence of My Best-Beloved in His Kingdom of Glory. Such is the Divine decree, if ye know it. Followers of Muḥammad! If it be your wish to riddle with your shafts the breast of Him Who hath caused His Book the Bayán to be sent down unto you, lay hands on Me and persecute Me, for I am His Well-Beloved, the revelation of His own Self, though My name be not His name.[274]

Consider also the passage from the Báb quoted in the note on **Primal Will** at 104 above, which cites this same tradition in its explanation.

161 **statements . . . made by 'Alí** These are recorded in the books of Muslim traditions and closely parallel the statement of Muḥammad, 'I am the first Adam . . .' See also Íqán, para. 178–9 for related sayings of 'Alí.

161 **'Muḥammad is our first . . .'** Tradition attributed to the Imám 'Alí in the Biḥár (see note 272 below).

164 **Divine Elixir**

I beg of Thee, O my God, by Thy most exalted Word which Thou hast ordained as the Divine Elixir unto all who are in Thy realm, the Elixir through whose potency the crude metal of human life hath been transmuted into purest gold . . .[275]

The Book of God is wide open, and His Word is summoning mankind unto Him. No more than a mere handful, however, hath been found willing to cleave to His Cause, or to become the instruments for its promotion. These few have been endued with the

Divine Elixir that can, alone, transmute into purest
gold the dross of the world, and have been empow-
ered to administer the infallible remedy for all the ills
that afflict the children of men.[276]

165 **copper . . . to the state of gold** Bahá'u'lláh further
elaborates this point in a later Tablet:

> Consider the doubts which they who have joined
> partners with God have instilled into the hearts of
> the people of this land. 'Is it ever possible', they ask,
> 'for copper to be transmuted into gold?' Say, Yes, by
> my Lord, it is possible. Its secret, however, lieth
> hidden in Our Knowledge. We will reveal it unto
> whom We will. Whoso doubteth Our power, let him
> ask the Lord his God, that He may disclose unto him
> the secret, and assure him of its truth. That copper
> can be turned into gold is in itself sufficient proof that
> gold can, in like manner, be transmuted into copper,
> if they be of them that can apprehend this truth.
> Every mineral can be made to acquire the density,
> form, and substance of each and every other mineral.
> The knowledge thereof is with Us in the Hidden
> Book.[277]

Shoghi Effendi also explains:

> Considering that a century ago, nobody knew the
> nature of matter, and couldn't split any kind of atom,
> it should not surprise the scientist that 'Abdu'l-Bahá
> states that copper can be transmuted into gold.
>   There may come a time, for all we know, when
> the mass of many atoms can be changed by scientists.
> We have no way of proving, or disproving at present
> the statement of 'Abdu'l-Bahá. Just because we cannot
> demonstrate a contention in the Bahá'í Teachings,
> does not mean the contention is not true.
>   The same holds true of the statement of Bahá'u-
> 'lláh in the Íqán, regarding transmutation of copper
> into gold after seventy years, under certain condi-
> tions.

We as Bahá'ís must assume that, as He had access
to all knowledge, He was referring to a definite
physical condition which theoretically might exist.
Because we don't know what this condition is in
scientific terms, does not refute Bahá'u'lláh's statement at all.[278]

171 **Point of the Bayán . . . likened the Manifestations** In
the Persian Bayán the Báb elaborates on the present
theme:

> It is clear and evident that the object of all preceding
> Dispensations hath been to pave the way for the advent
> of Muḥammad, the Apostle of God. These, including
> the Muḥammadan Dispensation, have had, in their
> turn, as their objective the Revelation proclaimed by
> the Qá'im. The purpose underlying this Revelation,
> as well as those that preceded it, has, in like manner,
> been to announce the advent of the Faith of Him
> Whom God will make manifest. And this Faith – the
> Faith of Him Whom God will make manifest – in its
> turn, together with all the Revelations gone before
> it, have as their object the Manifestation destined to
> succeed it. And the latter, no less than all the Revela-
> tions preceding it, prepare the way for the Revelation
> which is yet to follow. The process of the rise and
> setting of the Sun of Truth will thus indefinitely
> continue – a process that hath had no beginning and
> will have no end.[279]

174 **'God was alone . . .'** Tradition attributed to Imám 'Alí
and others.

175 **'veils of glory'** The term 'veils of glory' (Arabic,
subuḥát jalál) attributed here to the Imám 'Alí, is from
the tradition of Kumayl (see note at 109 above). In the
course of the Imám's answer to the question 'What is
Truth?' he makes this reference to the 'veils of glory'.
In general this term refers to those obstacles or veils

which prevent people from recognizing the truth of the Manifestations of God. In the Íqán Bahá'u'lláh mentions several types of veils such as the 'Seal of the Prophets'. Such veils have occurred in previous Dispensations as well. The Jewish people expected the promised Messiah to be seated upon the throne of David and their literal interpretation of this reference prevented them from recognizing Jesus Christ.

178 **that bird of Heaven** The Imám 'Alí.

178 **Fáṭimih** Daughter of Muḥammad and entitled 'the Chaste One'. She was consort of 'Alí and the mother of Ḥasan and Ḥusayn, the second and third Imáms. She is comparable in rank to such immortal heroines as Sarah, Ásíyih, the Virgin Mary, Ṭáhirih and Bahíyyíh Khánum.[280]

178 **'A thousand Fáṭimihs I have espoused . . .'** Ḥadíth of Imám 'Ali.

178 **'Abdu'lláh** Father of Muḥammad, born circa 545 AD. He belonged to the Baní Háshim, the noblest clan of the Quraysh tribe, direct descendants of Abraham. He died when he was but 25 years old while on an expedition to Syria, shortly before the Prophet's birth. Muḥammad is reported to have said: 'I am the son of two who were offered in sacrifice' meaning his great ancestor Ishmael and His own father 'Abdu'lláh. For 'Abdu'l-Muttalib had made a vow that if God would permit him to find and open the well of Zemzem and should give him ten sons, he would sacrifice one of them. Accordingly, when he had obtained his desire in both respects, he cast lots on his sons. When the lot fell on Abdu'lláh, 'Abdu'l-Muttalib redeemed him by offering a hundred camels.[281]

179 **battle of Khaybar** In the latter part of His ministry, following His truce with the Meccans, Muḥammad still faced implacable hostility from the northern settlement of Khaybar. Despite the superior advantage of the Jewish leaders, some 20,000 strong, Muḥammad overcame the several fortified areas of the oasis with a force numbering only 1,400. Many of the Jews surrendered on the Prophet's conditions which allowed them to continue to work the lands if they would pay Him a yearly rent of half of their produce. See also note on **Khaybar** at 92 above.

179 **my father** In other words 'Alí, whose prowess and courage during the battle of Khaybar are greatly extolled in the traditional accounts.

182 **attainment unto the presence of His Beauty**

> Regarding your question – This reference in the Íqán refers to the Meeting with Bahá'u'lláh. It will not be applicable again until another Manifestation of God appears, in at least 1,000 years from Bahá'u'lláh.[282]

The question posed concerned the above reference and asked whether such an 'attainment' finished with Bahá'u'lláh's Ascension, thereby depriving men of such a bounty forevermore. See also Íqán, paras. 148–51.

182 **But apart from all these things . . .** The powerful passage which begins with these words may be said to foreshadow Bahá'u'lláh's later enunciation in the Kitáb-i-Aqdas of the 'doctrine of the "Most Great Infallibility" of the Manifestation of God' which asserts that such infallibility is 'the inherent and exclusive right of the Prophet'.[283]

182 **'God doeth whatsoever He willeth . . .'** Cf. Qur'án 3:39; 22:14, 18.

182 **'All things lie imprisoned . . . '** This ḥadíth has been cited in a number of Bahá'u'lláh's Tablets. In one of the them He identifies the source as the Commander of the Faith, the Imám 'Alí.

182 **'Whoso sayeth "why" or "wherefore"'** Cf. Persian Bayán II:16.

182 **'He shall not be asked of His doings'** Compare with:

> Blessed is the man that hath acknowledged his belief in God and in His signs, and recognized that 'He shall not be asked of His doings'. Such a recognition hath been made by God the ornament of every belief and its very foundation. Upon it must depend the acceptance of every goodly deed. Fasten your eyes upon it, that haply the whisperings of the rebellious may not cause you to slip.[284]

184 **'He will, however, respite them . . .'** Cf. Qur'án 56:50.

187 **judged by their countenance** Compare with:

> All faces are dark except the face which is a mirror of the light of the love of divinity. This light is not accidental – it is eternal. It is not temporal but real. When the heart hath become clear and pure then the face will become illuminated, because the face is the mirror of the heart.[285]

> It is very strange that when a face is not illumined with the light of the love of God it is dark. When you look into it the traces of the divine glad-tidings are not manifest, but when the lights of God shine upon it, it becomes bright and enlightened, as it is said, 'In their faces you shall see the verdancy of paradise, and in their countenances is the sign of worship.'[286]

188 **Abode of Peace** See note on Baghdád at 22 above.

189 **'That all sorts of men . . .'** Cf. Qur'án 2:60, 7:160.

194 **'I am the servant of God.['] [']I am but a man like you.'** Qur'án 19:31, 18:110.

196 **I am God!** Compare with:

> Divinity, whenever I mention it, indicateth My complete and absolute self-effacement. This is the station in which I have no control over mine own weal or woe nor over my life nor over my resurrection.[287]

> When I contemplate, O my God, the relationship that bindeth me to Thee, I am moved to proclaim to all created things 'verily I am God!'; and when I consider my own self, lo, I find it coarser than clay![288]

> That Bahá'u'lláh should, notwithstanding the overwhelming intensity of His Revelation, be regarded as essentially one of these Manifestations of God, never to be identified with that invisible Reality, the Essence of Divinity itself, is one of the major beliefs of our Faith – a belief which should never be obscured and the integrity of which no one of its followers should allow to be compromised.[289]

197 **breeze of God** Consider how Bahá'u'lláh repeatedly punctuates the Íqán with these powerful expressions of the greatness of His own dawning Revelation. Concerning the divine breezes, He later revealed:

> No breeze can compare with the breezes of Divine Revelation, whilst the Word which is uttered by God shineth and flasheth as the sun amidst the books of men. Happy the man that hath discovered it, and recognized it, and said: 'Praised be Thou, Who art the Desire of the world, and thanks be to Thee, O Well-Beloved of the hearts of such as are devoted to Thee!'[290]

ANNOTATIONS TO THE ÍQÁN   163

198 **Guardianship** The question was asked, Is there any
reference to 'Abdu'l-Bahá or to the institution of the
Guardianship in the following quotation? '. . . Thus it
is that whatsoever be their utterance, whether it pertain to the realm of Divinity, Lordship, Prophethood,
Messengership, Guardianship, Apostleship or Servitude, all is true, beyond a shadow of a doubt'. . . Also,
are there any Manifestations to whom the titles of
Servitude have been particularly applied? The response of the Guardian was:

> The passage you have quoted from the 'Íqán' refers
> to the Prophets only, and not to the Guardianship.
> All Divine Manifestations have a station of servitude;
> and the latter does not apply to one or some of them
> to the exclusion of the rest.[291]

199 **Trustees of the depositories of Knowledge** 'We
cannot be sure to whom Bahá'u'lláh refers as the
"trustees" of knowledge.'[292]

201 **'Knowledge is one point . . .'** Maxim attributed to
Imám 'Alí.

201 **'Knowledge is a light . . .'** Muḥammad.

203 **a certain man** Ḥájí Mírzá Karím Khán, one of the self-
proclaimed Shaykhí leaders after Siyyid Káẓim; author
of numerous works including a vicious attack on the
Bábí Faith written at the request of Náṣiri'd-Dín Sháh
(see *God Passes By*, p. 91). Also see note under **a one-
eyed man** at 276 below.

203 **'Knowledge is all that is knowable . . .'** Tradition
attributed to the Imám Ṣádiq.

203 **Mi'ráj** 'Ascent'; used with reference to Muḥammad's celestial vision or 'night-journey' through the seven heavens. See Qur'án 17:1.

203 **'But for Thee, I would not have created the spheres.'** Tradition said to have been revealed through the Imám 'Alí.

204 **'Flingest thou thy calumnies . . .'** Cited from the Mathnaví of Rúmí.

204 **'All human attainment . . .'** Cited from the Mathnaví of Rúmí.

205 **'The most grievous of all veils . . .'** Traditional Ṣúfí saying. Although translated differently here, this is the same verse found in 76.

205 **'veils of glory'** See note at 175 above.

208 **alchemy** While condemning alchemy in its popularized form, Bahá'u'lláh Himself, in a number of Tablets on the subject, later undertook to explain its inner meanings. Note His own reference to such a possibility five lines below the reference to alchemy.

208 **We still bear the scar of chains** Bahá'u'lláh was imprisoned in the Síyáh-Chál of Ṭihrán for four months in 1852. During this period while His neck was 'weighed down by a mighty chain', He received the intimation of His prophetic Mission. Scars from the 'galling' weight of the two chains, called Qará Guhar and Salásil, remained with Him the rest of His days. See *God Passes By*, p. 101.

209 **Karím** Honourable; here an ironic reference to Ḥájí Mírzá Karím Khan.

210 **Sámirí** A magician who tempted the Israelites to the worship of the Golden Calf (Qur'án 20:90). After this violation he became an outcast wanderer.

213 **no remnant of either love or hate**

> We must never take one sentence in the Teachings and isolate it from the rest: it does not mean we must not love, but we must reach a spiritual plane where God comes first and great human passions are unable to turn us away from Him. All the time we see people who either through the force of hate or the passionate attachment they have to another person, sacrifice principle or bar themselves from the Path of God . . . We must love God, and in this state a general love for all men becomes possible. We cannot love each human being for himself, but our feeling towards humanity should be motivated by our love for the Father who created all men.[293]

213 **detach himself from the world of dust** 'Abdu'l-Bahá explains the prerequisites of a detached soul, saying, 'that he should not seek out anything whatever for his own self in this swiftly-passing life, but that he should cut the self away, that is, he should yield up the self and all its concerns on the field of martyrdom, at the time of the coming of the Lord'.[294]

214 **treasure the companionship** Compare with:

> O Friend! In the garden of thy heart plant naught but the rose of love, and from the nightingale of affection and desire loosen not thy hold. Treasure the companionship of the righteous and eschew all fellowship with the ungodly.[295]

214 **avoid fellowship with evil doers** This admonition also appears in the *Hidden Words*. As to the meaning of this subject, Shoghi Effendi advised in a letter written on

his behalf: 'In the passage "eschew all fellowship with the ungodly", Bahá'u'lláh means that we should shun the company of those who disbelieve in God and are wayward. The word "ungodly" is a reference to such perverse people.'[296]

216 **confer such new life**   As exalted as this new life may be, such a station should be viewed in relation to the limitations imposed upon the human spirit and its essential dependence on the Manifestations of God. The following extract defines an important difference in this regard:

> As regards to the passage No. 13 of the Arabic Hidden Words: that which Bahá'u'lláh declares we can find abiding within us is the power of the Divine Spirit, the reflection of the light of His Revelation. This reflection of the Divine Spirit, however, can in no way be compared to the Revelation which God discloses to His Prophets and Messengers. The similarity in the terminology should not confuse this distinction which is most fundamental.[297]

216 **stations of absolute certitude**   These stations or degrees of certitude are known traditionally in Islám as three: the certitude of knowing (e.g. to know or hear about fire), the certitude of seeing (to see fire) and the light of certitude (to experience burning).

218 **Hyacinth . . . Rose . . . Nightingale**   Probably allusions to the Manifestation of God.

218 **a thousand years**   '. . . as to the meaning of the passage in the "Íqán" in which Bahá'u'lláh refers to the renewal of the "City of God" once in about a thousand years: this, as the word about implies, is simply an approximate date, and should not therefore be taken literally.'[298]

Concerning your question relative to the duration of the Bahá'í Dispensation. There is no contradiction between Bahá'u'lláh's statement in the Íqán about the renewal of the City of God once every thousand years, and that of the Guardian in the Dispensation to the effect that the Bahá'í cycle will extend over a period of at least 500,000 years. The apparent contradiction is due to the confusion of the terms cycle and dispensation. For while the Dispensation of Bahá'u'lláh will last for at least one thousand years, His Cycle will extend still farther, to at least 500,000 years.

The Bahá'í cycle is, indeed, incomparable in its greatness. It includes not only the Prophets that will appear after Bahá'u'lláh, but all those who have preceded Him ever since Adam. These should, indeed, be viewed as constituting but preliminary stages leading gradually to the appearance of this supreme Manifestation of God.[299]

219 **Pentateuch** The Greek name given to the first five books of the Old Testament which are commonly ascribed to Moses and known also as the Torah.

219 **Gospel** Jesus Christ's ministry and teachings as recorded in the first four books of the New Testament: Matthew, Mark, Luke and John.

219 **Bayán** The Persian Bayán:

> . . . that monumental repository of the laws and precepts of the new Dispensation and the treasury enshrining most of the Báb's references and tributes to, as well as His warning regarding, 'Him Whom God will make manifest' . . . Peerless among the doctrinal works of the Founder of the Bábí Dispensation . . . this Book, of about eight thousand verses, occupying a pivotal position in Bábí literature, should be regarded primarily as a eulogy of the Promised One rather than a code of laws and ordinances designed to be a permanent guide to future generations.[300]

219 **Him Whom God will make manifest** The principal title used by the Báb to formally designate Bahá'u'lláh. The Báb also alluded to Bahá'u'lláh as the 'Abhá Horizon' and specifically recorded His title 'Bahá'u-'lláh' in a passage of the Persian Bayán wherein He eulogizes His 'Order'. See *God Passes By*, pp. 97–8.

219 **His own Book** The Kitáb-i-Aqdas, Bahá'u'lláh's Most Holy Book, 'that priceless treasury enshrining for all time the brightest emanations of the mind of Bahá'u'lláh, the Charter of His World Order, the chief repository of His laws, the Harbinger of His Covenant, the Pivotal Work containing some of His noblest exhortations, weightiest pronouncements, and portentous prophecies'.[301] The Kitáb-i-Aqdas was revealed about 1873, a decade after the Íqán. This present allusion to the Aqdas is mentioned by Shoghi Effendi in *God Passes By*, pp. 215–16.

219 **bread of heaven** See note on **bread** at 5 and 22 above.

222 **My Family** Shoghi Effendi defines the institution of the Imamate, the twelve lawful Successors of Muḥammad, as 'the repository of one of the two most precious legacies of Islám'.[302]

224 **Alif. Lám. Mím.** These and other disconnected letters appear at the head of 29 Súrihs of the Qur'án. Bahá'u-'lláh revealed a commentary on their meanings. See Taherzadeh, *The Revelation of Bahá'u'lláh*, vol. 1, pp. 125–6.

226 **divinely-revealed verses** With regard to His own verses, Bahá'u'lláh further states in the Lawḥ-i-Dunyá (Tablet of the World),

> Through each and every one of the verses which the Pen of the Most High hath revealed, the doors of love and unity have been unlocked and flung open to the face of men . . . Every verse which this Pen hath revealed is a bright and shining portal that discloseth the glories of a saintly and pious life, of pure and stainless deeds.[303]

Consider how amply these affirmations are demonstrated by the contents of the Íqán itself.

226 **'Urvatu'l-Vuthqá** See note at 28 above.

230 **'Marvel not if in the Qur'án . . .'** From a Persian poem of Sana'i.

236 **Joseph** An inspired Messenger of God in the Qur'án; son of Jacob. See also Íqán p. 254. In a passage of the Súriy-i-Damm, Bahá'u'lláh identifies Himself spiritually with Joseph. See Bahá'u'lláh, *Gleanings from the Writings of Bahá'u'lláh*, p. 89.

239 **Kawthar** See note at 25 above.

240 **Prophets 'endowed with constancy'** The term 'endowed with constancy' in regard to the Manifestations of God signifies that a Book was revealed to them. This is explained in para. 245 of the text. See also Shoghi Effendi, *World Order*, pp. 111 and 124.

242 **people of the Book** See note at 15 above.

248 **Mullá Ḥusayn**

> . . . the first Letter of the Living, surnamed the Bábu'l-Báb (the Gate of the Gate); designated as the 'Primal Mirror'; on whom eulogies, prayers and visiting Tablets of a number equivalent to thrice the

volume of the Qur'án had been lavished by the pen of the Báb; referred to in these eulogies as 'beloved of My Heart'; the dust of whose grave, that same Pen had declared, was so potent as to cheer the sorrowful and heal the sick; whom 'the creatures, raised in the beginning and in the end' of the Bábí Dispensation, envy, and will continue to envy till the 'Day of Judgement' . . . [304]

See also numerous references in *The Dawn-Breakers*.

248 **Siyyid Yaḥyá** (Siyyid Yaḥyáy-i-Dárábí)   Surnamed Vaḥíd, a distinguished Muslim divine who after three successive interviews with the Báb recognized Him and arose to champion His Cause. He was eventually martyred at Nayríz on 29 June 1850, just ten days before the execution of the Báb. See *Dawn-Breakers*, p. 173, and 'The commotion [in S̲h̲íráz after the return of the Báb from His pilgrimage] had assumed such proportions . . . Nayríz upheaval.'[305]

248 **Mullá Muḥammad 'Alíy-i-Zanjání**

Another famous advocate of the Cause of the Báb, even fiercer in zeal than Vaḥíd, and almost as eminent in rank, was Mullá Muḥammad-'Alíy-i-Zanjání, surnamed Ḥujjat. An Ak̲h̲bárí, a vehement controversialist, of a bold and independent temper of mind, impatient of restraint, a man who had dared condemn the whole ecclesiastical hierarchy . . . he had more than once, through his superior talents and fervid eloquence, publicly confounded his orthodox S̲h̲í'ah adversaries. Such a person could not remain indifferent to a Cause that was producing so grave a cleavage among his countrymen. The disciple he sent to S̲h̲íráz to investigate the matter fell immediately under the spell of the Báb. The perusal of but a page of the Qayyúmu'l-Asmá', brought by that messenger to Ḥujjat, sufficed to effect such a transformation within him that he declared, before the assembled 'ulamás of his native city, that should the Author of that work pronounce day to be night and the sun to be a shadow he would unhesitatingly uphold his verdict.[306]

Martyred together with 1,800 fellow-disciples in the upheaval at Zanján in 1850. See *The Dawn-Breakers*, chapter 24.

248 **Mullá 'Alíy-i-Bastámí**

> . . . energetic and audacious . . . one of the Letters of the Living, 'the first to leave the House of God (Shíráz) and the first to suffer for His sake'. . . excommunicated, chained, disgraced, imprisoned, and, in all probability, done to death.[307]

See also *Dawn-Breakers*, p. 89.

248 **Mullá Sa'íd-i-Bárfurúshí** According to *Nabíl's Narrative* he was one of those who fought at Shaykh Tabarsí.

248 **Mullá Yúsuf-i-Ardibílí** One of the 18 Letters of the Living. See *Dawn-Breakers*, pp. 187, 367, 399.

248 **Mullá Mihdíy-i-Khu'í** One of the 18 Letters of the Living; martyred at Shaykh Tabarsí.

248 **Siyyid Ḥusayn-i-Turshízí** One of the Seven Martyrs of Ṭihrán, a former mujtahid. See *Dawn-Breakers*, pp. 455–6.

248 **Mullá Mihdíy-i-Kandí** Martyred at Shaykh Tabarsí.

248 **Mullá Báqir** Another of the Letters of the Living. He was from Tabríz. See *Dawn-Breakers*, pp. 368, 505.

248 **Mullá 'Abdu'l-Kháliq-i-Yazdí** A S͟hayk͟hí divine and author of numerous works, mentioned in *Nabíl's Narrative*.

248 **Mullá 'Alíy-i-Baraqání** A paternal uncle of Ṭáhirih; a prominent S͟hayk͟hí divine renowned for his zealous devotions.

248 **'Guarded Tablet'** Understood to be a reference to God's knowledge.

249 **Kawt͟har** See note at 25 above.

254 **'O Son of Man! Many a day . . .'** Bahá'u'lláh, *Hidden Words*, Arabic no. 62.

254 **the light of beauty** Compare this passage with the following words of Bahá'u'lláh: 'the revelations of Thy matchless Beauty have at all times been imprinted upon the realities of all beings, visible and invisible'.[308]

256 **Mustag͟hát͟h** 'He Who is invoked'; the numerical value of which has been assigned by the Báb as the limit of the time fixed for the advent of the promised Manifestation, i.e. Bahá'u'lláh.

> During the Báb's confinement in the fortress of C͟hihríq . . . the Lawḥ-i-Ḥurúfat (Tablet of the Letters) was revealed, in honour of Dayyán – a Tablet which, however misconstrued at first as an exposition of the science of divination, was later recognized to have unravelled, on the one hand, the mystery of the Mustag͟hát͟h, and to have abstrusely alluded, on the other, to the nineteen years which must needs elapse between the Declaration of the Báb and that of Bahá'u'lláh.[309]

See also Nabíl's statement concerning Bahá'u'lláh's

explanation of the mystery of the Musta<u>gh</u>á<u>th</u>, which was revealed in answer to a request made of Him while He was in 'Akká:

> Bahá'u'lláh adduced from the statements of the Báb irrefutable evidence proving that the appearance of the Man-Yu<u>zh</u>iruhu'lláh [He Whom God will make manifest] must needs occur no less than nineteen years after the Declaration of the Báb. The mystery of the Musta<u>gh</u>á<u>th</u> had long baffled the most searching minds among the people of the Bayán and had proved an unsurmountable obstacle to their recognition of the promised One. The Báb had Himself in that Tablet unravelled that mystery; no one, however, was able to understand the explanation which He had given. It was left to Bahá'u'lláh to unveil it to the eyes of all men.[310]

256 **'Such is the bounty of God . . .'** Qur'án 57:21.

258 **Qayyúmu'l-Asmá'** The Báb's Commentary on the Súrih of Joseph from the Qur'án. See *God Passes By*, p. 23, for an outline of this Book's contents. Shoghi Effendi states that its 'fundamental purpose was to forecast what the true Joseph (Bahá'u'lláh) would, in a succeeding Dispensation, endure at the hands of one who was at once His arch-enemy and blood brother'. The work comprises 'above nine thousand three hundred verses' and is 'divided into one hundred and eleven chapters, each chapter a commentary on one verse of the above-mentioned súrih'.[311]

258 **His own martyrdom** The Báb was publicly martyred in Tabríz on 9 July 1850 (28 <u>Sh</u>a'bán 1266 AH) 'during the thirty-first year of His age and the seventh of His ministry'.[312] In the Kitáb-i-Panj-<u>Sh</u>a'n, one of His last works, He had alluded to the fact that the sixth Naw-

Rúz after the declaration of His mission would be the last He was destined to celebrate on earth.[313]

258 **Remnant of God** Baqíyyatu'lláh; Title applied both to the Báb and Bahá'u'lláh; here an allusion to Bahá'u-'lláh. This quotation is from chapter 58 of the Qayyúmu'l-Asmá'; for context see *Selections from the Writings of the Báb*, p. 59.

260 **'God is powerless . . .'** Cf. Qur'án 5:64.

261 **'Two verses have made Me old'** Traditional saying of Muḥammad with reference to two Qur'ánic verses: 'Be thou steadfast as thou hast been bidden' (11:112) and 'For this cause summon thou them, and be steadfast as thou hast been bidden' (42:15).

262 **Sadrih of the Riḍván of God** A reference to the youthful Báb, characterized as the 'Sadrih' or 'Tree', a symbol often used in relation to the Manifestation of God.

262 **Finally, He surrendered His soul** 'The more He exhorted them, the fiercer grew their enmity, till, at the last, they put Him to death with shameful cruelty. The curse of God be upon the oppressors!'[314] The Báb, the Prophet-Herald of the Bahá'í Faith, was executed by military firing squad at the barracks square of Tabríz in the northwest province of present-day Iran on 9 July 1850. For an account of the mysterious circumstances of that tragic event see Shoghi Effendi, *God Passes By*, pp. 52–4.

263 **that eternal Beauty revealed Himself** Shoghi Effendi has elaborated on the Bahá'í belief concerning the station of the Báb and its twofold reality as follows:

That the Báb, the inaugurator of the Bábí Dispensation, is fully entitled to rank as one of the self-sufficient Manifestations of God, that He has been invested with sovereign power and authority, and exercises all the rights and prerogatives of independent Prophethood, is yet another fundamental verity which the Message of Bahá'u'lláh insistently proclaims and which its followers must uncompromisingly uphold. That He is not to be regarded merely as an inspired Precursor of the Bahá'í Revelation, that in His person, as He Himself bears witness in the Persian Bayán, the object of all the Prophets gone before Him has been fulfilled, is a truth which I feel it my duty to demonstrate and emphasize . . . There can be no doubt that the claim to the twofold station ordained for the Báb by the Almighty, a claim which He Himself has so boldly advanced, which Bahá'u'lláh has repeatedly affirmed, and to which the Will and Testament of 'Abdu'l-Bahá has finally given the sanction of its testimony, constitutes the most distinctive feature of the Bahá'í Dispensation.[315]

267 **'And when the Standard of Truth . . .'** Tradition attributed to the Imám Ṣádiq, cited in the Bihár (see note 272 below).

267 **'One hour's reflection . . .'** Muḥammad.

269 **Prayer of Nudbih** See note at 33 above.

269 **'Where is He Who is preserved . . .'** Imám Mihdí, the twelfth Imám, in the Prayer of Nudbih.

269 **Abú-'Abdi'lláh** Designation of the sixth Imám, Ja'far-i-Ṣádiq (the Veridical); great-grandson of the Imám Ḥusayn. Died 765 AD, poisoned and martyred by the Abbásid Caliph, Manṣúr.

269 **Mihdí** The Guided One, i.e. the 'Hidden Imám', the promised Deliverer of S͟hí'í Islám. See further explanation concerning the Mihdí (or Mahdí) in 'Regarding S͟hí'í Islám' in chapter 2 of this study guide.

269 **'He will perform . . .'** A tradition from Abú-'Abdi'lláh, that is, Imám S̤ádiq.

270 **'Aválim** Short for *'Aválim'ul-Ulúm va'l-Ma'árif*, a compilation of S͟hí'í traditions, consisting of 100 volumes, collected by S͟hayk͟h 'Abdu'lláh Ibn Núru'lláh Baḥrayní, one of the distinguished students of Majlisí (see note on **Biháru'l-Anvár** at 272 below); also known as *Jám'í al-Ulúm va'l-Ma'árif*.

270 **Baní-Hás͟him** The clan of the Qurays͟h tribe from which Muḥammad appeared and the Báb was a descendant.

270 **a new Book** S͟hoghi Effendi identifies this as the Persian Bayán, stating that it fulfils 'the Muḥammadan prophecy that "a Youth from Baní- Hás͟him . . . will reveal a new Book and promulgate a new Law"'.[316]

270 **Hás͟himite Light** Allusion to the Báb's descent from Muḥammad and the Baní-Hás͟him clan.

271 **Arba'ín** Another collection of traditions.

271 **'Out of Baní-Hás͟him . . .'** Tradition of the Imám S̤ádiq.

272 **Biháru'l-Anvár** Literally, 'Seas of Lights'; an important collection of S͟hí'í traditions compiled in some 14 volumes by Muḥammad Báqiru'l-Majlisí at the close of the 16th century AD.

272 **'Aválim** See note at 270 above.

272 **Yanbú'** Collection of sacred traditions related to the Imáms, compiled by Muḥammad bin Aḥmad bin Junayd Abú-'Alí al-Khátib, known as Iskáfí (died 381 AH/991 AD). Iskáf was once a village in Mesopotamia. Iskáfí was buried in Rayy.

272 **'Knowledge is twenty and seven letters'** Hadíth of the Imám Ṣádiq.

> Regarding the passage beginning with the words: 'Knowledge consists of twenty-seven letters': this should not be interpreted literally. It only indicates the relative greatness and superiority of the new Revelation.[317]

> As to your question whether another letter will be added to our alphabet in order to have 27 letters, this tradition, in which reference to 27 letters is made, has no relation to the western alphabet.[318]

273 **Káfí** Short for the *Uṣul al-Káfí*, the most celebrated and reliable Shí'í collection of hadíth. It consists of three parts and includes 16,199 traditions related to the Imáms. Compiled by Muḥammad Ibn Ya'qúb Kulayní (died 328 AH/939 AD).

273 **Jábir** Jábir Ibn-i-Ḥayyán, pupil of the Imám Ṣádiq who compiled a book of the Imám's sayings. The importance of his tradition cited here is again emphasized in *God Passes By*, p. 80.

273 **Job** Prophet who dwelt in the land of Uz. See accounts of His life and sufferings in the Book of Job in the Old Testament, and in the Qur'án 21:83–4; 38:41–4.

273 **Daylamites** Here a reference to a group of Persian slaves serving as soldiers under their leader Daylam (hence Daylamites). The Persians, including the Daylamites, suffered heavy losses in an early battle with the Muslims at Al-Qádisíya, 15 AH/636 AD.

274 **Rawḍiy-i-Káfí** Title of the third part of the *Uṣul al-Káfí* (see 273 above).

274 **Muʻávíyih** Son of Vahháb; cited in the line of transmission of this traditional saying of the sixth Imám.

274 **Abú-ʻAbdiʼlláh** The Imám Ṣádiq. See note at 269 above.

274 **'Knowest thou Zawrá?'** Ḥadíth of Imám Ṣádiq.

276 **Bayán** See notes at 1 and 219 above.

276 **Mustagháth** See note at 256 above.

276 **a one-eyed man** Not authoritatively identified, but some students presume this to be a reference to 'the inordinately ambitious and hypocritical Ḥájí Mírzá Karím Khán, who at the special request of the Sháh had in a treatise viciously attacked the new Faith and its doctrines'.[319] Siyyid Kázim, when the former was one of his disciples, confidentially prophesied his future enmity to the Báb, stigmatizing him as 'the antichrist of the promised Revelation'. He was both one-eyed and sparsely bearded. After the Declaration of the Báb, he claimed the leadership of the Shaykhís. See Íqán, para. 203 and *Dawn-Breakers*, pp. 39–40.

276 **one who is reputed** Matches the position and subsequent actions of Mírzá Yaḥyá.

277 **In these days . . . in the future** Shoghi Effendi refers to this passage as describing 'the virulence of the jealousy which, at that time, was beginning to bare its venomous fangs'.[320]

278 **We betook ourselves to the wilderness** See description of Bahá'u'lláh's withdrawal to the mountains of Sulaymáníyyih in *God Passes By*, pp. 112, 120–6 and Balyuzi, *Bahá'u'lláh, King of Glory*, pp. 113–22.

279 **Amidst them all . . . unto Us.** This passage was added in Bahá'u'lláh's own hand to the original manuscript written out by 'Abdu'l-Bahá. See section 2 of this study.

279 **Primal Point** One of the principal titles of the Báb. He Himself proclaims: 'I am the Primal Point from which have been generated all created things.'[321]

279 **'Sufficient Witness is God unto Us.'** Qur'án 4:79, 166; 10:29; 13:43.

279 **'There is no power nor strength but in God alone.'** Source undetermined.

279 **'We are God's, and to Him shall we return.'** Qur'án 2:156. See Íqán. para. 99.

281 **Mufaḍḍal** A contemporary of the Imám Ṣádiq who transmitted traditions.

281 **'In the year sixty . . .'** Tradition of the Imám Ṣádiq.

282 **Bihár** Short for *Biháru'l-Anvár*. See note at 272 above.

282 **'In our Qá'im . . .'** Tradition attributed to several Imáms in the Bihár.

282 **'God indeed shall make whom He will to hearken . . .'**
Cf. Qur'án 35:22.

283 **'God verily will test them and sift them.'** Tradition
from the Imám Ṣádiq.

283 **'Every knowledge hath seventy meanings . . .'** Ḥadíth.

283 **'We speak one word . . .'** Tradition attributed to the
Imám Maʻṣúm, in the Bihár.

285 **none . . . yearning for the Truth** Baháʼuʼlláh, in a
later work, confirms:

> The generality of mankind is still immature. Had it
> acquired sufficient capacity We would have bestowed
> upon it so great a measure of Our knowledge that all
> who dwell on earth and in heaven would have found
> themselves, by virtue of the grace streaming from
> Our pen, completely independent of all knowledge
> save the knowledge of God, and would have been
> securely established upon the throne of abiding
> tranquillity.[322]

288 **the 'Bá'' and the 'Há''** Meaning Baháʼuʼlláh by use of
the first two letters of His Name. See Taherzadeh,
Revelation of Baháʼuʼlláh, vol. 1, p. 83, for a discussion.

Materials Related to the Study of the Íqán

Nine Purposes Defined in the Íqán

1. God's tests 8

2. Creation 28

3. Symbolic terms 53

4. Changes of ordinances 55

5. Manifestation of God 103

6. Prophets of God 128

7. Learning 153

8. Reading Scripture 185

9. Revelation 270

The Three Stages of Divine Revelation

1. *The Universal Revelation of God* (Tajallíy-i-'Ám)

- '. . . the light of divine knowledge and heavenly grace hath illumined and inspired the essence of all created things . . .' (28)

- '. . . whatever is in the heavens and whatever is on the earth is a direct evidence of the revelation within it of the attributes and names of God, inasmuch as within every atom are enshrined the signs that bear eloquent testimony to the revelation of that most great Light.' (107)

- '. . . it is clear and evident that such revelation already existeth in all things.' (149)

- 'We have demonstrated that all things are the recipients and revealers of the splendours of that ideal King, and that the signs of the revelation of that Sun, the Source of all splendour, exist and are manifest in the mirrors of beings.' (149)

- '. . . all created things eloquently testify to the revelation of that inner Light within them.' (149)

2. *The Specific Revelation of God* (Tajallíy-i-Kháṣṣ)

- 'Most Holy Outpouring' (Fayḍ-i-Aqdas) in the terminology of certain Ṣúfís. (150)

- '. . . it hath been eternally in the divine Knowledge.' (150)

- '. . . this revelation is confined to the innermost Essence, unto which no man can attain.' (150)

3. *The Secondary Revelation of God* (Tajallíy-i-Thání)

- 'Holy Outpouring' (Fayḍ-i-Muqqadas) in the terminology of some Ṣúfís. (151)

- '. . . this is admittedly applicable to the world of creation, that is, in the realm of the primal and original manifestation of God.' (151)

- 'Such revelation is confined to His Prophets and chosen Ones, inasmuch as none mightier than they hath come to exist in the world of being.' (151)

- 'Through them is transmitted a grace that is infinite, and by them is revealed the light that can never fade.' (106)

- '. . . all else besides these Manifestations, live by the operation of their Will, and move and have their being through the outpourings of their grace.' (109)

Biblical Quotations in the Íqán

Some of the quotations from the Bible employed in the Íqán have been cited exactly while others have been paraphrased or alluded to indirectly. It is helpful to remember that Bahá'u'lláh drew these verses from the standard Arabic version of the Bible which prevailed in the East. He then rendered their meaning in Persian for the convenience of the reader. Shoghi Effendi's translation of both into English throws additional light on the original intention of the verses. In other words, we have here Bahá'u'lláh's own translation of the literal meaning of the verses and then His elucidation of their true significance and purpose.

Isaiah 65:25
    'The wolf and the lamb shall feed together.' (119)

Matthew 2:2
    'Where is He that is born King of the Jews? for we have seen His star in the east and are come to worship Him!' (70)

Matthew 3:1–2
    'John the Baptist was preaching in the wilderness of Judea, and saying, Repent ye: for the Kingdom of heaven is at hand.' (70)

Matthew 8:22
    'Let the dead bury their dead.' See also Luke 9:60. (126)

Matthew 9:5–6

Cf. 'Arise from thy bed; thy sins are forgiven thee.' See also Mark 2:9–11 and Luke 5:23–4. (145)

Matthew 24:29–31

'Immediately after the oppression of those days shall the sun be darkened, and the moon shall not give her light, and the stars shall fall from heaven, and the powers of the earth shall be shaken: and then shall appear the sign of the Son of man in heaven: and then shall all the tribes of the earth mourn, and they shall see the Son of man coming in the clouds of heaven with power and great glory. And he shall send his angels with a great sound of a trumpet.' See also Mark 13:26 and Luke 21:27. (24, 66, 74, 79, 86)

Matthew 26:64

Cf. 'Beholdest thou not the Son of Man sitting on the right hand of power and might?' See also Mark 14:62. (144)

Mark 2:9–10

'Whether is it easier to say to the sick of the palsy, arise, and take up thy bed, and walk; or to say, thy sins are forgiven thee? that ye may know that the Son of Man hath power on earth to forgive sins.' (145)

Luke 9:60

'And it came to pass that on a certain day the father of one of the disciples of Jesus had died. That disciple reporting the death of his father unto Jesus, asked for leave to go and bury him. Whereupon, Jesus, that Essence of Detachment, answered and said: "Let the dead bury their dead."' (126)

Luke 21:33
'Heaven and earth shall pass away: but My words shall
not pass away.' (26)

John 3:5–6
'Except a man be born of water and of the Spirit, he
cannot enter into the Kingdom of God. That which
is born of the flesh is flesh; and that which is born of
the Spirit is spirit.' (125)

John 3:7
'Ye must be born again.' (125)

John 14:28
'I go away and come again unto you.' Cf. John
14:16–18, 16:12–14. (19, 20)

Qur'ánic Quotations in the Íqán

The inclusion in the Íqán of so many verses from the holy
Qur'án serves as an excellent introduction to that book for
readers who may not already be familiar with it. One very
useful exercise is to read these verses in the context of their
original setting in the Súrihs or chapters of the Qur'án.
Note that both translations and verse numbering vary from
edition to edition, which may require extra searching and
comparison on the part of the student. As yet there is no
common standard among scholars, either Muslims or
others, for the numbering of the verses. Rodwell's verse
numbering is used here and is generally found in footnotes
for Bahá'í publications. The súrihs, however, are numbered
according to the original Arabic rather than to Rodwell's
effort to place them in the order of their revelation.

Súrih of the Cow (Al-Baqara)

2:1   'Alif. Lám. Mím. No doubt is there about this
       Book: It is a guidance unto the God-fearing.' (224)

2:19   'They have thrust their fingers into their ears.'
       (175)

2:23   'And if ye be in doubt as to that which We have
       sent down to Our Servant, then produce a Súrah
       like it, and summon your witnesses, beside God,
       if ye are men of truth.' (226)

2:46   'They who bear in mind that they shall attain unto
       the Presence of their Lord, and that unto Him
       shall they return.' (148)

2:75   'A part of them heard the Word of God, and then,
       after they had understood it, distorted it, and
       knew that they did so.' (94)

2:79   'Woe unto those who, with their own hands, tran-
       scribe the Book corruptly, and then say: "This is
       from God", that they may sell it for some mean
       price.' (95)

2:85   'Believe ye then part of the Book, and deny part?'
       (181)

2:87   'As oft as an Apostle cometh unto you with that
       which your souls desire not, ye swell with pride,
       accusing some of being impostors and slaying
       others.' (13, 79)

2:89   'Although they had before prayed for victory over
       those who believed not, yet when there came unto
       them, He of Whom they had knowledge, they

disbelieved in Him. The curse of God on the infidels!' (159)

2:94   'Wish for death, if ye are men of truth.' (252)

2:115   'The East and the West are God's: therefore whichever way ye turn, there is the face of God.' (55)

2:136   'No distinction do We make between any of them.' (191)

2:143   'We did not appoint that which Thou wouldst have to be the Qiblih, but that We might know him who followeth the Apostle from him who turneth on his heels.' (55)

2:144   'We behold Thee from above, turning Thy face to heaven; but We will have Thee turn to a Qiblih which shall please Thee.' (54)

2:148   'All have a quarter of the Heavens to which they turn.' (245)

2:149   'Turn Thou Thy face towards the sacred Mosque.' (54)

2:156   'We are God's, and to Him shall we return.' (279)

2:176   'There is no piety in turning your faces toward the east or toward the west, but he is pious who believeth in God and the Last Day.' (101)

2:189   'They are periods appointed unto men.' (200)

2:210   'What can such expect but that God should come

down to them overshadowed with clouds?' (83, 152)

2:249   'They who held it as certain that they must meet God, said, "How oft, by God's will, hath a small host vanquished a numerous host!"'(148)

2:253   'Some of the Apostles We have caused to excel the others. To some God hath spoken, some He hath raised and exalted. And to Jesus, Son of Mary, We gave manifest signs, and We strengthened Him with the Holy Spirit.' (191; also first line only, 110)

2:285   'No distinction do We make between any of His Messengers!' (161)

Súrih of the Family of 'Imrán (Al'Imrán)

3:7   'None knoweth the meaning thereof except God and them that are well-grounded in knowledge.' (16) 'None knoweth the interpretation thereof but God and they that are well-grounded in knowledge.' (237)

3:28   'God would have you beware of Himself.' (105)

3:39   'God announceth Yaḥyá to thee, who shall bear witness unto the Word from God, and a great one and chaste.' (70)

3:70   'O people of the Book! Why disbelieve the signs of God to which ye yourselves have been witnesses?' (15)

3:71   'O people of the Book! Why clothe ye the truth with falsehood? Why wittingly hide the truth?' (15)

3:99 'Say, O people of the Book! Why repel believers from the way of God?' (15)

3:119 'And when they meet you, they say, "We believe"; but when they are apart, they bite their fingers' ends at you, out of wrath. Say: "Die in your wrath!" God truly knoweth the very recesses of your breasts.' (84)

3:182 'Already have Apostles before me come to you with sure testimonies, and with that of which ye speak. Wherefore slew ye them? Tell me, if ye are men of truth.' (157)

3:183 'Verily, God hath entered into a covenant with us that we are not to credit an apostle until he present us a sacrifice which fire out of heaven shall devour.' (157)

Súrih of the Women (An-Nisá')

4:45 'They pervert the text of the Word of God.' (92)

Súrih of the Table (Al-Má'ida)

5:2 '. . . and ordaineth whatsoever He pleaseth.' (103)

5:62 'Say, O people of the Book! do ye not disavow us only because we believe in God and in what He hath sent down to us, and in what He hath sent down aforetime, and because most of you are doers of ill?' (242)

5:67 '"The hand of God", say the Jews, "is chained up." Chained up be their own hands! And for that which they have said, they were accursed. Nay, outstretched are both His hands!' (147)

5:117   'Lord, send down upon us Thy bread from heaven.' (22)

Súrih of the Cattle (Al-An'ám)

6:7   'And had We sent down unto Thee a Book written on parchment, and they had touched it with their hands, the infidels would surely have said "This is naught but palpable sorcery."' (244)

6:35   'But if their opposition be grievous to Thee – if Thou canst, seek out an opening into the earth or a ladder into heaven.' (116)

6:59   'There is neither a thing green nor sere but it is noted in the unerring Book.' (210)

6:91   'Say: It is God; then leave them to entertain themselves with their cavillings.' (43) 'Leave them to entertain themselves with their cavillings!' (146)

6:103   'No vision taketh in Him, but He taketh in all vision; He is the Subtile, the All-Perceiving.' (104) 'No vision taketh in Him, but He taketh in all vision.' (182)

6:122   'Shall the dead, whom We have quickened, and for whom We have ordained a light whereby he may walk among men, be like him, whose likeness is in the darkness, whence he will not come forth?' (129)

6:127   'For them is an Abode of Peace with their Lord! and He shall be their Protector because of their works.' (188)

Súrih of Al-A'ráf

7:57   'In a rich soil, its plants spring forth abundantly by permission of its Lord, and in that soil which is bad, they spring forth but scantily.' (211)

7:145   'And if they see the path of righteousness, they will not take it for their path; but if they see the path of error, for their path will they take it. This, because they treated Our signs as lies, and were heedless of them.' (111)

7:178   'Hearts have they, with which they understand not, and eyes have they with which they see not!' (119) 'Hearts have they with which they understand not.' (125)

Súrih of the Spoils (Al-Anfál)

8:17   'Those shafts were God's, not Thine!' (196)

8:32   'If this be the very truth from before Thee, rain down stones upon us from heaven.' (230)

Súrih of Repentance (At-Tawba)

9:33   'Fain would they put out God's light with their mouths: But God hath willed to perfect His light, albeit the infidels abhor it.' (134, 136) 'God hath willed to perfect His light.' (99)

Súrih of Johan (Yúnus)

10:25   'And God calleth to the Abode of Peace; and He guideth whom He will into the right way.' (188)

Súrih of Húd

11:7   'And if thou shouldst say, "After death ye shall surely be raised again", the infidels will certainly exclaim, "This is nothing but manifest sorcery."' (121)

11:18   'The curse of God be upon the people of tyranny.' (12) Cf. 'God's malison on the head of the people of tyranny!' (135)

11:27   'Then said the chiefs of His people who believed not, "We see in Thee but a man like ourselves; and we see not any who have followed Thee except our meanest ones of hasty judgement, nor see we any excellence in you above ourselves: nay, we deem you liars."' (246)

11:38   'And as often as a company of His people passed by Him, they derided Him. To them He said: "Though ye scoff at us now, we will scoff at you hereafter even as ye scoff at us. In the end ye shall know."' (7)

11:61,62
    'And unto the tribe of Ṯẖamúd We sent their brother Ṣáliḥ. "O my people," said He, "Worship God, ye have none other God beside Him . . ." They made reply: "O Ṣáliḥ, our hopes were fixed on thee until now; forbiddest thou us to worship that which our fathers worshipped? Truly we misdoubt that whereunto thou callest us as suspicious."' (10)

11:113 'Be thou steadfast as thou hast been bidden.' (261)

Súrih of the Thunder (Ar-R'ad)

13:2   'He ordereth all things. He maketh His signs clear, that ye may have firm faith in attaining the presence of your Lord.' (148)

13:5   'If ever thou dost marvel, marvellous surely is their saying, "What! When we have become dust, shall we be restored in a new creation?"' (121)

13:41   'What He pleaseth will God abrogate or confirm: for with Him is the Source of Revelation.' (155)

Súrih of Abraham (Ibráhím)

14:24   'Seest thou not to what God likeneth a good word? To a good tree; its root firmly fixed, and its branches reaching unto heaven: yielding its fruit in all seasons.' (22)

14:27   'Verily God doeth whatsoever He willeth . . .' (103)

14:48   'On the day when the earth shall be changed into another earth.' (49)

Súrih of Al-Ḥijr

15:72   'As Thou livest, O Muḥammad! they are seized by the frenzy of their vain fancies.' (146)

Súrih of the Bee (An-Naḥl)

16:43   'Ask ye, therefore, of them that have the custody of the Scriptures, if ye know it not.' (212)

16:61   'If God should chastise men for their perverse doings, He would not leave upon the earth a moving thing! But to an appointed time doth He respite them.' (182)

Súrih of the Night Journey (Al-Isrá')

17:44   'Neither is there aught which doth not celebrate His praise.' (149)

17:51   'Erelong will they wag their heads at Thee, and say, "When shall this be?" Say: "Perchance it is nigh."' (123)

17:85   'And they will ask Thee of the Spirit. Say, "the Spirit proceedeth at My Lord's command."' (201)

Súrih of the Cave (Al Kahf)

18:110   'I am but a man like you.' (194)

18:111   'Let him then who hopeth to attain the presence of his Lord work a righteous work.' (148)

Súrih of Mary (Maryam)

19:22   'O would that I had died ere this, and been a thing forgotten, forgotten quite!' (59)

19:28   'O sister of Aaron! Thy father was not a man of wickedness, nor unchaste thy mother.' (59)

19:31   'I am the servant of God.' (194)

Súrih of Tá' Há'

20:124   'And whoso turneth away from My remembrance, truly his shall be a life of misery.' (286)

Súrih of the Prophets (Al-Anbiyá')

21:23   'He shall not be asked of His doings.' (182)

Súrih of the Light (Núr)

24:35   'God is the light of the heavens and of the earth.'
         (99) 'Tree that belongeth neither to the East nor
         to the West.' (57)

Súrih of the Furqán

25:7   'And they have said: "What manner of apostle is
         this? He eateth food, and walketh the streets.
         Unless an angel be sent down and take part in His
         warnings, we will not believe."' (80) 'Why hath not
         an angel been sent down to him, so that he should
         have been a warner with Him?' (88)

25:25   'On that day shall the heaven be cloven by the
         clouds.' (80)

25:44   'Thinkest thou that the greater part of them hear
         or understand? They are even like unto the brutes!
         yea, they stray even further from the path!' (272)

Súrih of the Poets (Ash-Shu'ará')

26:19   'What a deed is that which Thou hast done! Thou
         art one of the ungrateful. He said: "I did it indeed,
         and I was one of those who erred. And I fled from
         you when I feared you, but My Lord hath given Me
         wisdom, and hath made Me one of His Apostles."'
         (57)

26:187   'Make now a part of the heaven to fall down upon
         us.' (230)

26:227 'And they who act unjustly shall soon know what lot awaiteth them!' (251)

Súrih of the Story (Al-Qaṣaṣ)

28:5   'And We desire to show favour to those who were brought low in the land, and to make them spiritual leaders among men, and to make of them Our heirs.' (155)

28:20   'O Moses! of a truth, the chiefs take counsel to slay Thee.' (57)

Súrih of the Spider (Al-'Ankabút)

29:2   'Do men think when they say "We believe" they shall be let alone and not be put to proof?' (8)

29:23   'As for those who believe not in the signs of God, or that they shall ever meet Him, these of My mercy shall despair, and for them doth a grievous chastisement await.' (148) 'As for those who believe not in the verses of God, or that they shall ever meet Him, these of My mercy shall despair, and these doth a grievous chastisement await.' (234)

29:51   'Is it not enough for them that We have sent down unto Thee the Book?' (100)

29:69   'Whoso maketh efforts for Us', 'In Our ways shall We assuredly guide him.' (215)

Súrih of the Confederates (Al-Aḥzáb)

33:40   'Muḥammad is not the father of any man among you, but He is the Messenger of God.' (196)

'Muḥammad is the Apostle of God and the Seal of the Prophets.' (181)

Súrih of Sheba (Sabá‘)

34:13   'And few of My servants are the thankful.' (255)

34:43   'And when Our clear verses are recited to them, they say, "This is merely a man who would fain pervert you from your father's worship." And they say, "This is none other than a forged falsehood."' (238)

Súrih of the Angels (Al-Malá'ika)

35:15   'O men! Ye are but paupers in need of God; but God is the Rich, the Self-Sufficing.' (143)

35:39   'And their unbelief shall only increase for the unbelievers their own perdition.' (9)

Súrih of Yá' Sín

36:20   'Follow ye, O people! the Messengers of God.' (176)

36:30   'O the misery of men! No Messenger cometh unto them but they laugh Him to scorn.' (4)

Súrih of Those Ranging in Ranks (Aṣ-Ṣáffát)

37:36   'And they say, "Shall we then abandon our gods for a crazed poet?"' (234)

37:173 'And verily Our host shall conquer.' (134, 136)

Súrih of Ṣád

38:67   'Say: it is a weighty Message, from which ye turn aside!' (238)

Súrih of the Troops (Az-Zumar)

39:67   'The whole earth shall on the Resurrection Day be but His handful, and in His right hand shall the heavens be folded together. Praise be to Him! and high be He uplifted above the partners they join with him!' (51)

Súrih of the Believer (Al-Mu'min)

40:5   'Each nation hath plotted darkly against their Messenger to lay violent hold on Him, and disputed with vain words to invalidate the truth.' (4)

40:28   'And a man of the family of Pharaoh who was a believer and concealed his faith said: "Will ye slay a man because he saith my Lord is God, when He hath already come to you with signs from your Lord? If he be a liar, on him will be his lie, but if he be a man of truth, part of what he threateneth will fall upon you. In truth God guideth not him who is a transgressor, a liar."' (12)

40:34   'And Joseph came to you aforetime with clear tokens, but ye ceased not to doubt of the message with which He came to you, until, when He died, ye said, "God will by no means raise up a Messenger after Him." Thus God misleadeth him who is the transgressor, the doubter.' (236)

Súrih of the Made Plain (Fuṣṣilat)

41:30   'They that say "Our Lord is God", and continue steadfast in His way, upon them, verily, shall the angels descend.' (43)

41:53   'We will surely show them Our signs in the world and within themselves.' (107)

Súrih of Ornaments (Az-Zukhruf)

43:22   'Verily we found our fathers with a faith, and verily, in their footsteps we follow.' (162)

43:36   'And whoso shall withdraw from the remembrance of the Merciful, We will chain a Satan unto him, and he shall be his fast companion.' (286)

Súrih of Smoke (Ad-Dukhán)

44:10   'On the day when the heaven shall give out a palpable smoke, which shall enshroud mankind: this will be an afflictive torment.' (84)

44:43–4
        'Verily, the tree of Zaqqúm shall be the food of the Athím.' (209)

44:49   'Taste this, for thou forsooth art the mighty Karím!' (209)

Súrih of the Hobbling (Al-Játhiya)

45:5   'Such are the verses of God: with truth do We recite them to Thee. But in what revelation will they believe, if they reject God and His verses?' (228)

45:6   'Woe to every lying sinner, who heareth the verses of God recited to him, and then, as though he heard them not, persisteth in proud disdain! Apprise him of a painful punishment.' (229)

45:8   'And when he becometh acquainted with any of Our verses he turneth them to ridicule. There is a shameful punishment for them!' (230)

45:22   'What thinkest thou? He who hath made a God of his passions, and whom God causeth to err through a knowledge, and whose ears and whose heart He hath sealed up, and over whose sight He hath cast a veil – who, after his rejection by God, shall guide such a one? Will ye not then be warned?' (237)

45:24   'And when Our clear verses are recited to them, their only argument is to say, "Bring back our fathers, if ye speak the truth!"' (231)

Súrih of the Victory (Al-Fatḥ)

48:10   'In truth, they who plighted fealty unto thee, really plighted that fealty unto God.' (196) 'The hand of God is above their hands.' (147)

Súrih of Qáf

50:15   'Are We wearied out with the first creation? Yet are they in doubt with regard to a new creation!' (121)

50:20   'And there was a blast on the trumpet, – lo! it is the threatened Day! And every soul is summoned to a reckoning, – with him an impeller and a witness.' (122)

Súrih of the Scatterers (Al-Dháriyát)

51:21   'And also in your own selves: will ye not then behold the signs of God?' (107)

51:22   'The heaven hath sustenance for you, and it containeth that which you are promised.' (75)

Súrih of the Moon (Al-Qamar)

54:6   'The day when the Summoner shall summon to a stern business.' (267)

54:50   'Our Cause is but one.' (161)

Súrih of the Merciful (Ar-Raḥmán)

55:5   'Verily, the sun and the moon are both condemned to the torment of infernal fire.' (36)

55:29   'Verily, His ways differ every day.' (74)

55:39   'On that day shall neither man nor spirit be asked of his Sin.' (186)

55:41   'By their countenance shall the sinners be known, and they shall be seized by their forelocks and their feet.' (186)

55:56   'whom no man nor spirit hath touched before' (78)

Súrih of Iron (Al-ḥadíd)

57:3   'the First and the Last, the Seen, and the Hidden' (151)

57:21   'Such is the bounty of God; to whom He will He giveth it.' (256)

Súrih of the Emigration (Al-Ḥashr)

59:2   'Wherefore, take ye good heed ye who are men of insight!' (256)

59:19   'And be ye not like those who forget God, and whom He hath therefore caused to forget their own selves.' (107)

Súrih of the Prohibition (At-Taḥrím)

67:2   'That He might prove you, which of you excel in deeds.' (39)

Súrih of the Steps (Al-Ma'árij)

70:40   'But nay! I swear by the Lord of the Easts and the Wests.' (45)

Súrih of Noah (Núh)

71:26   'Lord! Leave not upon the land a single dweller from among the unbelievers.' (7)

Súrih of the Shrouded One (Al-Muddaththir)

74:50   'Affrighted asses fleeing from a lion.' (55)

Súrih of Man (Al-Insán)

76:5   'The righteous shall drink of a cup tempered at the camphor fountain.' (41)

76:9   'We nourish your souls for the sake of God; we seek from you neither recompense nor thanks.' (22)

Súrih of the Great Announcement (Al-Naba')

78:29   'We noted all things and wrote them down.' (149)

Súrih of the Cleaving (Al-Infiṭár)

82:1   'When the heaven shall be cloven asunder.' (46)

List of Proper Names and Titles

This list provides a brief description of each of the proper names and titles found in the Íqán. A more detailed description can be found for most names in the annotations to the Íqán in chapter 6.

Aaron

The brother of Moses and his senior by three years, a Levite descended from 'Imrán (Amran). The priestly class of Judaism are his descendants. (59)

'Abdu'lláh

Father of Muḥammad, born circa 545 AD. He belonged to the Baní Háshim, the noblest clan of the Quraysh tribe, direct descendants of Abraham. He died while on an expedition to Syria, shortly before the Prophet's birth, at the age of 25. (178)

'Abdu'lláh-i-Ubayy

Pagan divine, prince, who was chief or head of the hypocrites. (114)

Abel and Cain

Sons of Adam. Although Abel was the stronger of the two and could easily have prevailed against his brother, he let Cain slay him for he would not stretch forth his hand against him.[323] (157)

Abú-'Abdi'lláh

Designation of the sixth Imám, Ja'far-i-Ṣádiq (the Veridical). (269, 274)

Abú-Ámir

Known as ar-Ráhib, the Hermit, because of earlier ascetic practices. A Medinian renegade who strongly opposed Muḥammad. (114)

Abú-Jahl

Muslim epithet meaning the 'Father of Ignorance'; his real name was Abú'l-Ḥakím, the 'Father of Wisdom'. One of the prominent Meccans who 'waxed relentless in his opposition and unbelief' to Muḥammad. (129)

Aḥmad-i-Aḥsá'í, Shaykh

Founder of the Shaykhí movement, he was the first of the 'twin resplendent lights' who heralded the Báb and Bahá'u-'lláh. (72)

'Alí

The first Imám and rightful successor of Muḥammad; cousin of the Prophet and husband of His daughter Fáṭimih. (127, etc.)

Amalekites

Expelled in early times from Babylonia, they spread through Arabia to Palestine, Syria and Egypt. Bitter opponents of Israel, they suffered a crushing defeat from Saul. (92)

Caiaphas, Joseph

The 'leading divine of that age', he presided at the court which condemned Jesus. (144)

David

Messenger of God, son of Jesse and second King of Israel; revealer of the Psalms. (55)

Daylamites

Inhabitants of the area of Daylamán, the present-day province of Gílán, with its capital in Ra<u>sh</u>t. Because of their resistance to the 'Abbásids, their name became synonymous with heterodoxy and heresy. (273)

Fáṭimih

Daughter of Muḥammad, consort of 'Alí; mother of Ḥasan and Ḥusayn, the second and third Imáms; entitled 'the Chaste One'. (178)

Gabriel

Archangel; the mediator of revelation to Muḥammad and the personification of the Divine Spirit to Him. (54, 92, 123, 174)

Ḥamzih

'Prince of Martyrs', Muḥammad's uncle, who was slain at the battle of Uhud by Waḥshi. (129)

Herod

King of Judaea, known as Herod the Great. He ordered the slaughter of infant boys around the time of the birth of Christ. (69)

Húd

Prophet of God sent to the people of 'Ád in Arabia.[324] (9)

Ḥusayn

The third Imám; son of 'Alí and Fáṭimih; the 'Prince of Martyrs', slain at Karbílá. His return is fulfilled in the appearance of Bahá'u'lláh. (135–40, 179, 251)

Ibn-i-Ṣúríyá

Rabbi chosen by the people of Khaybar at Muḥammad's request to cite a point of Jewish law. (92)

'Imrán (Amran)

His descendants include Moses and Aaron and constitute a subdivision of the priestly Levites. He was not literally Moses' father. (57)

Jábir

Jábir Ibn-i-Ḥayyán, pupil of the Imám Ṣádiq. He wrote a book of the Imám's sayings. (273)

Job

Prophet who dwelt in the land of Uz. (273)

John the Baptist

Divinely-appointed forerunner of Jesus Christ. Of priestly descent, his mother was cousin of the Virgin Mary. He baptized Jesus and was beheaded by Herod the Tetrarch. (70)

Joseph

Son of Jacob and an inspired Messenger of God in the Qur'án. (236, 282)

Kaʿb-Ibn-i-Ashraf

Medinian Jewish priest, poet and inveterate enemy of Muḥammad who conspired with Muḥammad's arch-enemy Abú Sufyán to bring about the Prophet's death. (114)

Karím

Honourable. In the Íqán, an ironic reference to Ḥájí Mírzá Karím Khán. (209)

Karím Khán, Ḥájí Mírzá

Self-proclaimed Shaykhí leader after Siyyid Káẓim. He was the author of many works including a vicious attack on the Bábí Faith written at the request of the Sháh.[325] (203–9)

Káẓim-i-Rashtí, Siyyid

The chief disciple and successor of Shaykh Aḥmad, he was

the second of the 'twin resplendent lights' who heralded the Báb and Bahá'u'lláh. (72)

Mary

The Virgin Mary, mother of Jesus Christ. (24, 59, 88, 141, 144, 191)

Mu'áviyih

Son of Vahháb; cited in the line of transmission of the traditional sayings of the sixth Imám. (274)

Mufaḍḍal

Contemporary of the Imám Ṣádiq who transmitted traditions.[326] (281)

Naḍr-Ibn-i-Ḥárith

One of 'nine persons who made mischief in the land',[327] because, it is said, he brought from Persia the romance of Rustam and Isfandiyar and recited it in the assemblies of the Quraysh. (114)

Nebuchadnezzar

King of Babylon who captured Jerusalem in 599 BC and destroyed it in 588. (92)

Nimrod

Ancient king of Babylon and persecutor of Abraham according to Muslim commentaries. (67)

Pharaoh

Title of the ancient rulers of Egypt; in the Íqán, the perse-cutor of Moses and His people. (12, 16, 57–8, 68, 92)

Pilate

Pagan Roman procurator of Judaea, 26–36 AD, who issued the death-sentence of Jesus Christ. (144)

Qá'im

Literally, 'He Who Ariseth'. The Promised One of Shí'í Islám. Refers to the Báb.

Rúz-bih

A Persian who embraced Christianity and later recognized Muḥammad. Later named Salmán. (71)

Ṣádiq

The sixth Imám. (86, 142, 270, 272, 275, 281, 283)

Ṣáliḥ

An ancient Prophet to the Arabs. (10)

Sámirí

A magician who tempted the Israelites to the worship of the Golden Calf[328] and afterwards became an outcast wanderer. (210)

Yaḥyá

In the Íqán, refers to John the Baptist, son of Zachariah. Yaḥyá is Arabic for John. (70)

Yaḥyá, Siyyid

Surnamed Vaḥíd, a distinguished Muslim divine who became a Bábí and was martyred at Nayríz on 29 June 1850, ten days before the execution of the Báb. (248)

Zachariah

Father of John the Baptist; of priestly descent from Aaron. (70)

Words Most Often Used by Bahá'u'lláh in the Íqán (based on the English translation)

Word	Count	Word	Count
God	740	book	89
Divine	249	earth	88
people	225	heart	81
Qur'án	180	Muḥammad	81
knowledge	174	verses	79
truth	172	man	75
day	139	grace	71
revelation	131	being	66
heaven	116	understanding	66
revealed	111	Prophets	65
words	107	glory	64
men	106	meaning	63
manifest	98	verse	63
light	96	life	62
sun	91	mysteries	59

Word	Count	Word	Count
power	59	dispensation	47
beauty	55	traditions	47
spirit	55	age	45
signs	54	Manifestation	45
soul	54	presence	45
souls	52	word	43
divines	50	attain	42
testimony	50	sovereignty	42
Manifestations	49	days	41
Jesus	48	law	41
wisdom	48	Lord	41

Symbolic Terms Explained in the Íqán

The purpose of the symbolic terms used by the Messengers of God is set out in the Íqán itself in paragraph 53. Attentive consideration of the various meanings assigned to these terms will greatly assist the student in understanding similar scriptural references both of the past and the present.

1. *'Oppression' – 'essential feature of every Revelation'* (28–30)

   • men oppressed and afflicted
   • lingering traces of the Sun of Truth vanish
   • reins of mankind in hands of the foolish
   • portals of divine unity and understanding closed
   • certain knowledge replaced by idle fancy
   • corruption usurps station of righteousness
   • want of capacity to acquire spiritual knowledge

2. *'Sun' and 'moon' – manifold meanings intended* (31–45)

   • Suns of Truth, the universal Manifestations of God

- Prophets of God, the saints, and their companions
- divines of former Dispensation
- annulment of laws and teachings of previous Dispensations such as prayer and fasting

3. *'Cleaving of the heavens'* (46)

- former Dispensation superseded and annulled

4. *'Changing of the earth'* (48–51)

- transformation of the 'earth' of human hearts

5. *'Sign of the Son of man in heaven'* (66–73)

- in the visible heaven: a star will appear
- in the invisible heaven: a harbinger will be made manifest

6. *'Heaven'* (74–5)

- loftiness and exaltation of the Manifestations
- many and diverse applications such as: heaven of Command, heaven of Will, heaven of Divine Purpose, etc.

7. *'Clouds' 'of heaven-sent trials'* (79–83)

- things contrary to the ways and desires of men
- annulment of laws
- abrogation of former Dispensations
- repeal of rituals and customs current amongst men
- appearance of the Manifestation in the image of mortal man with human limitations

8. *'Smoke'* (84)

- grave dissensions
- abrogation and demolition of recognized standards
- utter destruction of narrow-minded exponents of such standards

9. *'Angels'* (86–7)

- holy beings who have consumed all human traits and limitations and clothed themselves with spiritual attributes

10. *'Perverting'* the text (92–7)

- interpretation in accordance with the idle imaginings and vain desires of the divines

11. *'Wolf'* and the *'lamb'* (119)

12. *'Life'* and *'death'* (120)

- life of faith – the heavenly and everlasting life
- death of unbelief

13. *'Trumpet'* (122–3)

- trumpet-call of a new Revelation

14. *'Day of Resurrection'*, *'Day of Judgement'* (122–4, 141–3)

15. *'Ascendancy'*, *'power'* and *'authority'* (136)

16. *'Riches'* (143)

- independence of all else but God

17. *'Poverty'* (143)

   • lack of things that are of God

18. *'Presence of God'* (151)

   • presence of the Manifestations of God

19. *'Return'* (157–60)

20. *'Seal of the Prophets'* (172, 181, 196, 237)

21. *'First'* and *'last'* (172–4)

22. *'Veils of glory'* (174–8)

   • misunderstood terms and allusions in scripture
   • divines and doctors that reject the new Manifestations

23. *'Spirit'* (201)

Index of Figures of Speech used Symbolically

Flame(s)
  of the burning Bush 62
  of divine wisdom 12
  of God's burning Bush 148
  of His love 262
  of His loving mention 214
  hottest, in the heart 129
  of love 226
  of nethermost fire 17
  of undying Fire 141
  of utter detachment 75

Flower(s)
  mystic 211
  of Riḍván of heavenly reunion 64

Food 22, 23, 209
  cometh from heaven 23
  conferreth everlasting life 22
  is bread of heaven 219
  tree of Zaqqúm shall be, of Athím 209

Fount
  of certitude 167

Fountain
  the camphor fountain 41
  of divine inspiration 76

Fountain-head
  of infinite grace 82
  of knowledge 16

Fragrance
  of belief 86
  of the Beloved's utterance 158

Regarding Divine Tests

All the quotations appearing here are taken from the Íqán.

> . . . from time immemorial even unto eternity the Almighty
> hath tried, and will continue to try, His servants, so that
> light may be distinguished from darkness, truth from
> falsehood, right from wrong, guidance from error, happi-
> ness from misery, and roses from thorns. Even as He hath
> revealed: 'Do men think when they say "We believe" they
> shall be let alone and not be put to proof?' (8)

Two Kinds of Divine Tests: Words and Deeds

> Were men to meditate upon the lives of the Prophets of
> old, so easily would they come to know and understand the
> ways of these Prophets that they would cease to be veiled
> by such deeds and words as are contrary to their own
> worldly desires . . . (57)

As thou comest to comprehend the essence of these divine mysteries, thou wilt grasp the purpose of God, the divine Charmer, the Best-Beloved. Thou wilt regard the words and the deeds of that almighty Sovereign as one and the same; in such wise that whatsoever thou dost behold in His deeds, the same wilt thou find in His sayings, and whatsoever thou dost read in His sayings, that wilt thou recognize in His deeds. Thus it is that outwardly such deeds and words are the fire of vengeance unto the wicked, and inwardly the waters of mercy unto the righteous. Were the eye of the heart to open, it would surely perceive that the words revealed from the heaven of the will of God are at one with, and the same as, the deeds that have emanated from the Kingdom of divine power. (61)

THE WORDS

Know verily that the purpose underlying all these symbolic terms and abstruse allusions, which emanate from the Revealers of God's holy Cause, hath been to test and prove the peoples of the world; that thereby the earth of the pure and illuminated hearts may be known from the perishable and barren soil. From time immemorial such hath been the way of God amidst His creatures, and to this testify the records of the sacred books. (53)

Noah:

He several times promised victory to His companions and fixed the hour thereof. But when the hour struck, the divine promise was not fulfilled. This caused a few among the small number of His followers to turn away from Him
. . . (7)

THE DEEDS

. . . the appearance of that immortal Beauty in the image of mortal man, with such human limitations as eating and

drinking, poverty and riches, glory and abasement, sleep-
ing and waking, and such other things as cast doubt in the
minds of men, and cause them to turn away . . . Other
Prophets, similarly, have been subject to poverty and
afflictions, to hunger, and to the ills and chances of this
world. As these holy Persons were subject to such needs
and wants, the people were, consequently, lost in the wilds
of misgivings and doubts, and were afflicted with bewilderment and perplexity. (79–80)

Moses:

Consider how He hath suddenly chosen from among His
servants, and entrusted with the exalted mission of divine
guidance Him Who was known as guilty of homicide, Who,
Himself, had acknowledged His cruelty, and Who for well-
nigh thirty years had, in the eyes of the world, been reared
in the home of Pharaoh and been nourished at his table.
Was not God, the omnipotent King, able to withhold the
hand of Moses from murder, so that manslaughter should
not be attributed unto Him, causing bewilderment and
aversion among the people? (58)

Jesus:

How could she [Mary] claim that a Babe Whose father was
unknown had been conceived of the Holy Ghost? . . . And
now, meditate upon this most great convulsion, this grievous test. Notwithstanding all these things, God conferred
upon that essence of the Spirit, Who was known amongst
the people as fatherless, the glory of Prophethood, and
made Him His testimony unto all that are in heaven and
on earth. (59–60)

Muḥammad:

. . . the Voice of Gabriel was heard again: 'Turn Thou Thy
face towards the sacred Mosque.' In the midst of that same
prayer, Muḥammad suddenly turned His face away from

Jerusalem and faced the Ka'bih. Whereupon, a profound dismay seized suddenly the companions of the Prophet. Their faith was shaken severely. So great was their alarm, that many of them, discontinuing their prayer, apostatized their faith. Verily, God caused not this turmoil but to test and prove His servants. Otherwise, He, the ideal King, could easily have left the Qiblih unchanged, and could have caused Jerusalem to remain the Point of Adoration . . . (54)

* * *

Such things take place only that the souls of men may develop and be delivered from the prison-cage of self and desire . . . inasmuch as the divine Purpose hath decreed that the true should be known from the false, and the sun from the shadow, He hath, therefore, in every season sent down upon mankind the showers of tests from His realm of glory. (56)

The Fundamental Bahá'í Principles

These are all excerpts from the writings of Shoghi Effendi.

. . . the fundamental verity underlying the Bahá'í Faith, that religious truth is not absolute but relative, that Divine Revelation is not final but progressive.[329]

Its teachings revolve around the fundamental principle that religious truth is not absolute but relative, that Divine Revelation is progressive, not final.[330]

. . . the truth that in accordance with the principle of progressive revelation every Manifestation of God must needs vouchsafe to the peoples of His day a measure of divine guidance ampler than any which a preceding and less receptive age could have received or appreciated.[331]

. . . as different stages in the eternal history and constant evolution of one religion, Divine and indivisible, of which it itself forms but an integral part.[332]

. . . the fundamental principle which constitutes the bed-rock of Bahá'í belief, the principle that religious truth is not absolute but relative, that Divine Revelation is orderly, continuous and progressive and not spasmodic or final.[333]

. . . that from 'the beginning that hath no beginning' the Prophets of the one, the unknowable God, including Bahá'u'lláh Himself, have all, as the channels of God's grace, as the exponents of His unity, as the mirrors of His light and the revealers of His purpose, been commissioned to unfold to mankind an ever-increasing measure of His truth, of His inscrutable will and Divine guidance, and will continue to 'the end that hath no end' to vouchsafe still fuller and mightier revelations of His limitless power and glory.[334]

Bahá'u'lláh inculcates the basic principle of the relativity of religious truth, the continuity of Divine Revelation, the progressiveness of religious experience.[335]
. . . readily and gratefully recognizes their respective contributions to the gradual unfoldment of one Divine Revelation, unhesitatingly acknowledges itself to be but one link in the chain of continually progressive Revelations . . . [336]

The fundamental principle enunciated by Bahá'u'lláh . . . is that religious truth is not absolute but relative, that Divine Revelation is a continuous and progressive process, that all the great religions of the world are divine in origin, that their basic principles are in complete harmony, that their aims and purposes are one and the same, that their teachings are but facets of one truth, that their functions are complementary, that they differ only in the nonessential aspects of their doctrines, and that their missions represent successive stages in the spiritual evolution of human society.[337]

8

Index to the Íqán

The entries in this index are listed word by word, thus Daylamites follows Day of God. Numbers refer to paragraphs.

not withheld, 14
outpouring of, 197
transmitted through
Manifestations, 106
highest and most excel-
ling, 148
Guidance, 18, 217, 224

Ḥamzih, 129
Hatred, seeker must purge
heart of, 213
Haughtiness, 28
'Him Whom God will make
manifest', 219, 276
Heart,
cleansing of, 49, 77, 99,
204, 213
devoured by fire of the
tongue, 213
earth of the, 48–9
home of the Desire of the
world, 205
limitations of, 49
peace of, 65
pure, 5
seat of the revelation of the
mysteries of God, 213
surrender of, 64
understanding, 119, 125,
187
Heaven
cleaving of, 46
Qur'án likened to, 40
symbolic meaning of, 46,
51–2, 66, 74–5, 79
visible, 66
See also Paradise
Heedlessness, 5, 120, 148,
158, 182–5, 245, 249–50,
253–4
of the Báb's revelation,
112, 260, 239–42,
275-6

of Bahá'u'lláh's revelation,
281–2
of divines, see Divines
of humanity, 111–12, 133,
230–40, 242, 285
overcoming one's, 18
punishment of the heed-
less, 229–30
Hell, 123, 127
Herod, 69
Ḥijáz, 18, 71
Holiness, realm of, 5
Holy Spirit, 141
Húd, 9–10
Súrah of, 5
Human beings,
blindly follow leaders of
their Faith, 89, 175–6
capacities of, 107
display signs of God, 107
fail to recognize Manifestation of God, 3
God's gifts to, 23, 107
immortality of, see Immortality
limits of the, 2
nature of, 107, 109
nobility of, 109
reunion with God, 18, 44
signs of God in, see Signs,
of God
station of, 1, 149
transformation of, 163–4,
167
See also Humanity and Self
Humanity
the common people, 232
superiority of, 233
education of, 103
heedlessness of, see Heedlessness
leaders of, see Leaders
love for God, 31

oppression of, *see* Oppression, of humanity
perversity of, of this age, 14
petty-mindedness of, 14
relationship with God, 104–6
transformation of, 269–70
unity of, *see* Unity
See also Human being
Humility,
seeker must have, 213
Ḥúrís, 78
Ḥusayn, Imám (Prince of Martyrs), 135–6, 138–40, 179, 251
Ḥusayn, Mullá, 248
Ḥusayn-i-Turs͟hízí, Siyyid, 248
Hypocrisy, 28

Ibn-i-Ṣúríyá, 92
Imaginings, vain, 2, 14, 52
Imáms, 152, 161, 270–1, 284
Immortality, 2, 128, 167, 217
'Imrán, 57
Infidels, 118, 129, 242, 260
Iniquity, 29, 120
Interpretation, 16, 136–7, 237
literal, 25, 89, 122, 283–4
of scripture, 93, 125, 199
'Iráq, 18
Irs͟hádu'l-'Avám, 203
Islám, 25, 26, 98, 113, 114, 117, 156, 161, 170, 185, 242, 268
opposition to, 242
Israel, people of, 17, 68, 230
See also Jews

Jábir, 273

Jealousy, 277
Jerusalem, 54, 92
Jesus, 17, 19–21, 55, 60, 62, 88, 98, 125–6, 141, 144–5, 159, 161, 172, 191, 219, 236, 273, 282
birth of, 59, 69–70
prophecies of, 88
return of, 21
signs of, 24–6
Jews, 17, 19, 54, 92, 97, 144–5, 146–8, 230, 268
Jewish divines, *see* Divines, Jewish
See also Israel, people of
Job, 273
John, Gospel of St, 24
John the Baptist (Yaḥyá), 70
Joseph, 236, 282
Judea, 70
Judgement, 114, 120–1, 140
Day of, 118, 122
knowledge of, 130
signs of, 118
meaning of, 123, 128
of Muḥammad, 121
See also Tests
Justice, 16, 22

Ka'b-Ibn-i-As͟hraf, 114
Ka'bih, 54
Káfí, 273
Karbilá, 136
Karím K͟hán, Ḥájí Mírzá, 203–10
Káẓim-i-Ras͟htí, Siyyid, 72
K͟haybar, 92, 179
Kindness, 214
Kingdom of God, entrance into, 125
Kings, 117, 131
Knowledge, 16, 28, 56, 66, 73–4, 156

behaviour of, 5
between Jesus and the
present, 88
between Moses and
Muḥammad, 55
coming of, in this day, 63
denial of, 3–14, 125
distinction between, 191–5
failure to recognize, 3,
153–4
foretell coming of next
Manifestation, 13
greatness of, 228
independence of, 102
lives of, 57, 79–80
Messengership of, 196,
198
names of, 191
nature of, 74, 106, 160–2,
174, 178–80
one not elevated above the
rest, 110
oneness of, 20, 106,
161–2, 170–2, 191, 196
opposition to, 4–17, 157
of divines, 15, 79, 177,
238–40
motivation for, 13–15
passing of, 23
purpose of, 31, 103, 128
recognition of, 2, 27, 81–2,
151, 154–5, 241
excuses for lack of, 245
standard for, 244
rejection of, 120, 252–3
see also Heedlessness
relationship to God,
105–6, 109–10, 151,
193, 196–8
return of, 156, 160, 162,
168–71
seat of the revelation of

Essence of God, 27
signs heralding advent of,
16, 66–73
sovereignty of, 103,
113–14, 136, 140
station of, 32, 109, 140,
161, 191
sufferings of, 47, 80, 136,
157
Suns of Truth, 31
testimony of, 228
truth of, 201
Universal Manifestation,
187
ways of, contrary to ways of
humanity, 61
Mankind, see Humanity
Mark, Gospel of St, 24
Martyrs, 252
Bábí, 263, 275
Mary, mother of Jesus, 24, 59,
88, 141, 144, 191
Matthew, Gospel of St, 24
Mecca (Baṭḥá), 54, 93
Medina (Yathrib), 54, 93
Mercy, 22, 28, 120
Messiah, 17, 144, 147
Metaphysics, 203
Midian, 57
Mihdí, the, 269
Mihdíy-i-Kandí, Mullá, 248
Mihdíy-i-Khu'í, Mullá, 248
Miracles, 157, 230
Mi'ráj, 203–4
Moon
shall not give its light, 24,
41–2, 66
symbolic meaning of, 31,
52, 73, 200
Moses, 12, 17, 55, 62, 92,
147–8, 159, 161, 172,
210, 219, 230, 236,
273, 282

9

A Suggested Course of Study
for the Íqán

Outline of Lessons

1. *The Importance of the Íqán and its Study*

    Study Aids:
    Importance of the Íqán: Extracts
    Major Themes of the Íqán as set out by Shoghi
        Effendi in *God Passes By*
    List of Translations of the Íqán

2. *Historical Background for a Study of the Íqán*

    Study Aids:
    Historical Setting
    Shí'í Islám and the Bahá'í Faith
    Maternal Uncles of the Báb

3. *Additional Preparatory Materials*

    Study Aids:
    Notes on *God Passes By*, pp. 138–9
    Understanding the Divine Texts: Principles and
        Prerequisites

4. *Major Themes of the Íqán as set out by Shoghi Effendi*

    Study Aids:
    Major Themes with Suggested Paragraph References

Passages Cited in *The Dispensation of Bahá'u'lláh*
Passages Cited in *Gleanings from the Writings of
Bahá'u'lláh*
The Fundamental Bahá'í Principles

5. *Review of the Text*, Part I, paras. 1–53

Study Aids:
A Subject Outline of the Íqán
Annotations for paras. 1–53
Regarding Divine Tests
Question Sheet

6. *Review of the Text*, Part I, paras. 54–101

Study Aids:
Annotations for paras. 54–101
Question Sheet

7. *Review of the Text*, Part II, paras. 102–55

Study Aids:
The Three Stages of Divine Revelation
Annotations for paras. 102–55
Question Sheet

8. *Review of the Text*, Part II, paras. 156–212

Study Aids:
Annotations for paras. 156–212
Question Sheet

9. *Review of the Text*, Part II, paras. 213–90

Study Aids:
Annotations for paras. 213–90
Question Sheet

Related Assignments

Read the book.

Review the text, identifying paragraph references for the major themes set out by Shoghi Effendi.

Prepare your own subject outline or points for clarification in the review lessons.

Note down any questions or points for clarification in the review lessons.

List symbolic terms explained in the text along with the various meanings.

Compile a list of supplementary reading material.

Questions Related to the Text

Paras. 1–53

1. What initial prerequisites are given for the attainment of faith and certitude? (2)

2. What is Bahá'u'lláh's purpose in recounting the sufferings and indignities of the Prophets of old? (4-18)

3. Why does the Almighty continually try and test His servants? (9)

4. What are the causes of the people's denial and persecution of the Manifestations of God? (13–15ff)

5. What is the explanation of the Muḥammad's declaration: 'I am Jesus.'? (20)

6. What does Bahá'u'lláh refer to as the 'essential feature of every Revelation'? Explain its meaning. (31ff)

7. In what sense does the symbolic term 'sun' apply to the Manifestations of God? (31-3)

8. How do the terms 'sun' and 'moon' relate to the laws of prayer and fasting? (38–42)

9. Identify some of the qualities demonstrated by Bahá'u-'lláh in the example of teaching given in these passages. (40)

10. Explain the meaning of the 'cleaving of the heaven'. (46)

11. What is the purpose of the Prophets' use of symbolic terms and abstruse allusions? (53)

12. List the symbolic terms explained in the Íqán and give their several meanings, with paragraphs references.

Paras. 54–101

1. Describe the intimation Moses received of His divine mission. (57)

2. What 'twofold signs' have announced the Revelation of each of the Prophets of God? (66, 73)

3. What is Bahá'u'lláh's purpose in citing the records of past sacred books? (68)

4. What description does Bahá'u'lláh give of the inner state of the Manifestations of God? (74)

5. Describe the 'two kinds' of Knowledge mentioned by Bahá'u'lláh. (76)

6. Give four of the symbolic meanings of the term 'clouds'. (79–83)

7. What does Bahá'u'lláh foretell with regard to the future of the Cause of God? (85)

8. What is meant by 'angels'? (86–7)

9. Why have religious leaders denied the subsequent Manifestations of God? (88)

10. What does 'perverting the text' refer to? (93–6)

11. What warning does Bahá'u'lláh give to the people of the Bayán? (101)

Paras. 102–55

1. How much of the Divine Essence do the Manifestations of God comprehend? (105)

2. Find two ways in which Bahá'u'lláh characterizes the Imáms of S̲h̲í'í Islám. (113, 152, also 139)

3. How do the Manifestations differ from each other in revealing the divine names and attributes? (111)

4. What is meant by the undisputed sovereignty exercised by the Prophets of God during their time on earth? (114)

5. From what 'heaven' do the divine verses descend? (120, 129)

6. What does it mean to the 'born again'? (125)

7. Give a symbolic meaning of the term 'tomb'. (128)

8. What are the spiritual meanings of 'riches' and 'poverty'? (143)

9. What is the 'highest and most excelling grace' bestowed upon men? (138)

10. What are the three stages of divine revelation? (149–51)

11. What is the sole and fundamental purpose of all learning? (153)

Paras. 156–212

1. Give one of the reasons why the wayward of every age have attributed ignorance and folly to the Manifestations of God. (158)

2. In what sense do the scriptural references to the 're-turn' of the Prophets of old relate to the companions? (160, 170, etc)

3. Describe the twofold station of the Manifestations of God. (161–2, 191–5)

4. What is the 'Divine Elixir' and how does Bahá'u'lláh describe its potency and effects? (164–7)

5. Give two meanings for the term 'veils of glory'. (174–8)

6. What is the meaning of the 'Day of Resurrection'? (182)

7. What does Bahá'u'lláh state to be the purpose for the reading of scriptures and holy books? (185)

8. Why do the utterances of the various Manifestations of God appear at times to diverge and differ? (192)

9. How are the statements of the Prophets of God such as 'I am God!' to be understood and explained? (196)

10. What does Bahá'u'lláh state with regard to metaphysical abstractions, to alchemy and to natural magic? (203-8)

Paras. 213–90

1. What is Bahá'u'lláh's counsel with regard to backbiting? (214)

2. Name three categories of the signs of God. (217)

3. Explain the symbolic meaning of the term 'City'. (219)

4. What produces the 'chill of heedlessness' in the hearts of some people? (226)

5. Describe the 'spiritual disease' mentioned by Bahá'u-'lláh. (236)

6. Why does it mean to 'err through a knowledge'? (238)

7. What has been established in the Qur'án as a 'standard' for recognition of the Manifestations? (244)

8. Give three proofs demonstrating the truth of the mission of the Báb. (246–65)

9. Describe the character of the transformation which is the object of every Revelation. (270)

10. To what does the term 'Bání Háshim' refer? (270–1)

11. What is the purpose of each aspect of the 'twofold language' of the utterances of the Prophets of God? (283)

Bibliography

'Abdu'l-Bahá. *The Promulgation of Universal Peace.* Wilmette, Ill.: Bahá'í Publishing Trust, 1982.

— *Tablets of Abdul-Baha Abbas.* New York: Bahá'í Publishing Committee, vol. 2, 1940.

— *Tablets of the Divine Plan.* Wilmette, Ill.: Bahá'í Publishing Trust, 1977.

The Báb. *Selections from the Writings of the Báb.* Haifa: Bahá'í World Centre, 1976.

Bahá'í Prayers: A Selections of Prayers revealed by Bahá'u'lláh, the Báb and 'Abdu'l-Bahá. Wilmette, Ill.: Bahá'í Publishing Trust, 1991.

Bahá'í World, The. vol. 13. Haifa: The Universal House of Justice, 1970.

Bahá'í World Faith. Wilmette, Ill.: Bahá'í Publishing Trust, 2nd edn. 1976.

Bahá'u'lláh. *Epistle to the Son of the Wolf.* Wilmette, Ill.: Bahá'í Publishing Trust, 1988.

— *Gleanings from the Writings of Bahá'u'lláh.* Wilmette, Ill.: Bahá'í Publishing Trust, 1983.

— *The Hidden Words.* Wilmette, Ill.: Bahá'í Publishing Trust, 1990.

— *The Kitáb-i-Aqdas.* Haifa: Bahá'í World Centre, 1992.

— *Kitáb-i-Íqán.* Wilmette, Ill.: Bahá'í Publishing Trust, 1989.

— *Prayers and Meditations.* Wilmette, Ill.: Bahá'í Publishing Trust, 1987.

— *The Seven Valleys and the Four Valleys.* Wilmette, Ill.: Bahá'í Publishing Trust, 1991.

Balyuzi, H. M. *Bahá'u'lláh, The King of Glory.* Oxford: George Ronald, 1980.

Compilation of Compilations, The. Prepared by the Universal House of Justice 1963–1990. 2 vols. [Sydney]: Bahá'í Publications Australia, 1991.

The Dartmouth Bible.

Gail, Marzieh. *Dawn over Mount Hira.* Oxford: George Ronald, 1976.

Giachery, Ugo. *Shoghi Effendi: Recollections.* Oxford: George Ronald, 1973.

Goodall, Helen S. and Cooper, Ella Goodall. *Daily Lessons Received at 'Akká.* Wilmette, Ill.: Bahá'í Publishing Trust, 1979.

Hatcher, William S., and Martin, J. Douglas. *The Bahá'í Faith: The Emerging Global Religion.* San Francisco: Harper & Row, Publishers, 1984.

Holy Bible. King James Version. London: Collins, 1839.

The Koran. Trans. J.M. Rodwell. London: Dent, Everyman's Library, 1963.

The Koran. trans. Sale, 1870.

Lights of Guidance: A Bahá'í Reference File. Compiled by Helen Hornby. New Delhi: Bahá'í Publishing Trust, 2nd edn. 1988.

Living the Life. London: Bahá'í Publishing Trust, 1984.

Momen, Moojan. *An Introduction to Shí'í Islam.* London: Yale University Press, 1985.

Nabíl-i-A'ẓam. *The Dawn-Breakers: Nabíl's Narrative of the Early Days of the Bahá'í Revelation.* Wilmette, Ill.: Bahá'í Publishing Trust, 1970.

Sears, William. *Release the Sun.* Wilmette, Ill.: Bahá'í Publishing Trust, 1995.

— *Thief in the Night.* Oxford: George Ronald, 1961.

Shoghi Effendi. *Bahá'í Administration.* Wilmette, Ill.: Bahá'í Publishing Trust, 1968.

— *Dawn of a New Day: Messages to India 1923–1957.* New Delhi: Bahá'í Publishing Trust, 1970.

— *Directives from the Guardian.* New Delhi: Bahá'í Publishing Trust, 1973.

— *God Passes By.* Wilmette, Ill.: Bahá'í Publishing Trust, rev. edn. 1974.

— *High Endeavors: Messages to Alaska.* [Anchorage]: National Spiritual Assembly of the Bahá'ís of Alaska, 1976.

— *Letters from the Guardian to Australia and New Zealand.* Sydney, Australia: Bahá'í Publishing Trust, 1970.

— *The Light of Divine Guidance: The Messages from the Guardian of the Bahá'í Faith to the Bahá'ís of Germany and Austria.* 2 vols. Hofheim-Langenhain: Bahá'í-Verlag, 1982.

— *Messages to the Bahá'í World.* Wilmette, Ill.: Bahá'í Publishing Trust, 1971.

— *The Promised Day is Come.* Wilmette, Ill.: Bahá'í Publishing Trust, rev. edn. 1980.

— *The Unfolding Destiny of the British Bahá'í Community: The Messages of the Guardian of the Bahá'í Faith to the Bahá'ís of the British Isles.* London: Bahá'í Publishing Trust, 1981.

— *The World Order of Bahá'u'lláh.* Wilmette, Ill.: Bahá'í Publishing Trust, 1991.

Taherzadeh, Adib. *The Revelation of Bahá'u'lláh,* vol. 1. Oxford: George Ronald, 1974.

References

1. Shoghi Effendi, *God Passes By*, pp. 139, 140.
2. From a letter written on behalf of Shoghi Effendi to an individual, 11 March 1923, in *Compilation*, vol. 1, p. 212.
3. From a letter written on behalf of Shoghi Effendi to an individual believer, 14 June 1930, in *Light of Divine Guidance*, vol. 1, p. 37.
4. From a letter written on behalf of Shoghi Effendi to a National Spiritual Assembly, 28 June 1930, in the International Bahá'í Archives.
5. From a letter written on behalf of Shoghi Effendi to a Local Spiritual Assembly, 27 March 1931, in *Compilation*, vol. 1. p. 213.
6. From a letter written on behalf of Shoghi Effendi to an individual believer, 9 February 1932, in ibid. p. 215.
7. From a letter written on behalf of Shoghi Effendi to an individual believer, 9 June 1932, in ibid. p. 216.
8. From a postscript in the hand of Shoghi Effendi on a letter written on his behalf to an individual believer, 25 August 1932, in the Bahá'í International Archives.
9. From a letter written on behalf of Shoghi Effendi to an individual believer, 7 May 1933, in the Bahá'í International Archives.
10. From a letter written on behalf of Shoghi Effendi to an individual believer, 1 October 1933, in the Bahá'í International Archives.
11. From a transcript of a letter written on behalf of Shoghi Effendi to an individual believer, 7 August 1934, Bahá'í International Archives.
12. Bahá'u'lláh, *Kitáb-i-Íqán*, para. 185.
13. ibid. para. 233.
14. ibid. para. 77.
15. Gail, *Dawn Over Mount Hira*, pp. 112–13.
16. Bahá'u'lláh, *Kitáb-i-Aqdas*, para. 182.
17. 'Abdu'l-Bahá, *Promulgation*, p. 459.

18. From a letter written on behalf of Shoghi Effendi, 24 November 1932, *Compilation*, vol. 1, p. 32.
19. In the handwriting of Shoghi Effendi appended to a letter written on his behalf to an individual believer, 30 January 1925, in *Compilation*, vol. 1, p. 205.
20. Shoghi Effendi, *Unfolding Destiny*, p. 457.
21. From a letter written on behalf of Shoghi Effendi, 16 February 1932, in *Compilation*, vol. 1, p. 215.
22. Shoghi Effendi, *God Passes By*, pp. 138–9.
23. ibid. p. 138.
24. Bahá'u'lláh, *Kitáb-i-Íqán*, para. 251.
25. Shoghi Effendi, *God Passes By*, p. 149.
26. See Bahá'u'lláh, *Gleanings*, pp. 111, 115.
27. From a letter written on behalf of Shoghi Effendi to a National Spiritual Assembly, 17 February 1939, in *Dawn of a New Day*, p. 78.
28. Shoghi Effendi, *God Passes By*, p. 25.
29. The Báb, *Selections*, p. 104.
30. Bahá'u'lláh, *Epistle to the Son of the Wolf*, p. 18.
31. ibid. p. 44.
32. Bahá'u'lláh, *Kitáb-i-Aqdas*, para. 5.
33. Bahá'u'lláh, in *Compilation*, vol. 2, p. 245.
34. Daniel 12:4.
35. Daniel 12:9. See also *Some Answered Questions*, Chapter 10, 'Traditional Proofs Exemplified from the Book of Daniel'.
36. From a letter written on behalf of Shoghi Effendi to an individual believer, 21 April 1939, in *Lights of Guidance*, p. 477.
37. Shoghi Effendi, *World Order of Bahá'u'lláh*, p. 115.
38. Shoghi Effendi, Statement to the United Nations Commission on Palestine, 1947, cited in Preface to *Promised Day is Come*, p. v.
39. Shoghi Effendi, *God Passes By*, p. 220.
40. From a letter written on behalf of Shoghi Effendi to an individual believer, 28 July 1936, in *Directives of the Guardian*, pp. 51–2.
41. Hatcher and Martin, *The Bahá'í Faith*, pp. 3–5.
42. Shoghi Effendi, *God Passes By*, p. 47.
43. Nabíl, *Dawn-Breakers*, p. 446.
44. Balyuzi, *Bahá'u'lláh, King of Glory*, pp. 163–5.
45. Taherzadeh, *Revelation of Bahá'u'lláh*, vol. 1, pp. 158–9.
46. ibid. pp. 159.

47. Balyuzi, *Bahá'u'lláh, King of Glory*, p. 165.
48. Giachery, *Shoghi Effendi*, pp. 149–50.
49. Shoghi Effendi, *Dispensation*, p. 21 and Shoghi Effendi, *World Order of Bahá'u'lláh*, p. 113.
50. Shoghi Effendi, *Dispensation*, pp. 20–1 and Shoghi Effendi, *World Order of Bahá'u'lláh*, pp. 113–14.
51. Shoghi Effendi, *Dispensation*, p. 23 and Shoghi Effendi, *World Order of Bahá'u'lláh*, pp. 114–15.
52. Shoghi Effendi, *Dispensation*, p. 23 and Shoghi Effendi, *World Order of Bahá'u'lláh*, p. 115.
53. Shoghi Effendi, *Dispensation*, pp. 23–4 and Shoghi Effendi, *World Order of Bahá'u'lláh*, pp. 115–16.
54. Bahá'u'lláh, *Gleanings*, pp. 17–27.
55. ibid. pp. 46–9.
56. ibid. pp. 50–6.
57. ibid. pp. 177–9.
58. ibid. pp. 179–83.
59. ibid. pp. 264–70.
60. Shoghi Effendi, *Messages to the Bahá'í World*, p. 153. See also *Íqán*, para 256.
61. Bahá'u'lláh, *Íqán*, para. 48.
62. See *Íqán*, paras. 28, 48, 233, etc.
63. The Báb, *Selections*, pp. 77–8.
64. Cited in E. G. Browne's notes to the first English edition of *The Episode of the Báb*, p. 344.
65. Bahá'u'lláh, *Prayers and Meditations*, pp. 285–6.
66. Bahá'u'lláh, *Gleanings*, p. 242.
67. ibid. p. 105.
68. Bahá'u'lláh, *Kitáb-i-Aqdas*, para. 99.
69. Bahá'u'lláh, *Gleanings*, pp. 67–8.
70. ibid. p. 70. See also *Íqán* paras. 31, 74, 109.
71. ibid. p. 29.
72. ibid. p. 31.
73. ibid. pp. 198–9.
74. Luke 4:24.
75. Matt. 13:57.
76. Bahá'u'lláh, *Prayers and Meditations*, p. 325.
77. The Báb, *Selections*, p. 102.
78. Bahá'u'lláh, quoted in Shoghi Effendi, *God Passes By*, p. 98.
79. Bahá'u'lláh, *Hidden Words*, Persian no. 79.
80. See also *Íqán*, paras. 156, 178.
81. Bahá'u'lláh, *Gleanings*, p. 195.

82. 'Abdu'l-Bahá, *Tablets*, vol. 3, p. 677. See also *Íqán*, paras. 22, 92, 219, 230.
83. Bahá'u'lláh, *Gleanings*, pp. 57–8.
84. ibid. p. 76.
85. From a letter written on behalf of Shoghi Effendi to an individual believer, 28 October 1949, in *Lights of Guidance*, p. 508. See also *Íqán*, paras. 161–2.
86. From a letter written on behalf of Shoghi Effendi to an individual believer, 3 March 1957.
87. From a letter written on behalf of Shoghi Effendi to an individual, 26 January 1939.
88. Qur'án 7:73, 17:59.
89. See Tablet cited in *Qámús-i-Íqán* II, p. 1804, under Ṣáliḥ.
90. Bahá'u'lláh, *Epistle to the Son of the Wolf*, p. 83.
91. ibid. p. 130.
92. ibid. p. 103.
93. Bahá'u'lláh, *Gleanings*, pp. 56–7.
94. Qur'án 21:68–9 Sale's version; see also 29:24, 37:97–8.
95. Al-Beidawi, etc. cited by Sale, p. 321.
96. See Qur'án 21:68–70; 29:24; 37:97–8.
97. Shoghi Effendi, *God Passes By*, p. 107.
98. Gen. 11:28, 15:7.
99. Shoghi Effendi, *God Passes By*, p. 107.
100. Qur'án 7:107–8; see also 27:12.
101. Bahá'u'lláh, quoted in Shoghi Effendi, *God Passes By*, p. 169.
102. Shoghi Effendi, *Letters to Australia and New Zealand*, p. 41.
103. 'Abdu'l-Bahá, *Some Answered Questions*, p. 50.
104. Bahá'u'lláh, *Prayers and Meditations*, p. 150.
105. ibid. p. 76.
106. 'Abdu'l-Bahá, *Selections*, p. 207.
107. Bahá'u'lláh, *Gleanings*, pp. 57–8.
108. ibid. pp. 105–6.
109. ibid. pp. 68–9.
110. ibid. pp. 56–7.
111. Qur'án 2:113.
112. Bahá'u'lláh, *Prayers and Meditations*, p. 80.
113. Bahá'u'lláh, *Gleanings*, p. 272.
114. Bahá'u'lláh, *Hidden Words*, Arabic no. 44.
115. 'Abdu'l-Bahá, Tablet in the International Bahá'í Archives, Bahá'í World Centre.
116. II Peter 1:20.

117. The Báb, *Selections*, p. 118.
118. 'Abdu'l-Bahá, *Selections*, pp. 44–6.
119. 'Abdu'l-Bahá, *Some Answered Questions*, p. 144.
120. From a letter of the Universal House of Justice to an individual believer, 18 March 1974.
121. Taherzadeh, *Revelation of Bahá'u'lláh*, vol. 1, p. 152. See Shoghi Effendi, *God Passes By*, p. 141 and *Íqán*, para. 24.
122. From a letter written on behalf of Shoghi Effendi to an individual believer, 23 June 1948, in Shoghi Effendi, *Unfolding Destiny*, p. 451.
123. Bahá'u'lláh, *Gleanings*, p. 221. See 'Abdu'l-Bahá, *Some Answered Questions*, chapter 7.
124. Bahá'u'lláh, in *Bahá'í Prayers* (US), p, 211.
125. Shoghi Effendi, *God Passes By*, pp. 109–10. See also Qur'án 6:127, 10:26.
126. Bahá'u'lláh, *Hidden Words*, Persian no. 15.
127. Bahá'u'lláh, *Tablets*, p, 189.
128. Bahá'u'lláh, in *Bahá'í Prayers* (US), p. 212.
129. From a letter written on behalf of Shoghi Effendi to an individual believer, 29 November 1937, in *Lights of Guidance*, p. 492.
130. From a letter written on behalf of Shoghi Effendi to an individual believer, 7 February 1945, in *Lights of Guidance*, p. 419.
131. The Báb, *Selections*, p. 123.
132. Bahá'u'lláh, *Prayers and Meditations*, p. 318.
133. Footnote from Sale's translation of *The Koran*, p. 502.
134. Bahá'u'lláh, *Gleanings*, pp. 166–7.
135. ibid. p. 167.
136. Bahá'u'lláh, *Prayers and Meditations*, p. 57.
137. Quoted in Shoghi Effendi, *Promised Day is Come*, p. 99.
138. 'Abdu'l-Bahá, quoted in Shoghi Effendi, *God Passes By*, p. 238.
139. Bahá'u'lláh, *Prayers and Meditations*, p. 132.
140. Bahá'u'lláh, *Kitáb-i-Íqán*, para. 109.
141. ibid. para. 110.
142. Shoghi Effendi, *Promised Day is Come*, p. 108.
143. Shoghi Effendi, *World Order*, p. 102.
144. Bahá'u'lláh, *Epistle to the Son of the Wolf*, p. 90.
145. Bahá'u'lláh, quoted in Shoghi Effendi, *Promised Day is Come*, p. 111.
146. Shoghi Effendi, *Directives of the Guardian*, p. 27.

147. 'Abdu'l-Bahá, in *Compilation*, vol. 2, p. 232.
148. From a letter written on behalf of Shoghi Effendi to an individual believer, 4 January 1936, in *Compilation*, vol. 2, p. 238.
149. Qur'án 33:40.
150. Bahá'u'lláh, *Gleanings*, p. 60.
151. Bahá'u'lláh, *Seven Valleys*, p. 37.
152. Bahá'u'lláh, *Kitáb-i-Íqán*, para. 53.
153. Bahá'u'lláh, *Hidden Words*, Persian no. 7.
154. ibid. Persian no. 8.
155. Bahá'u'lláh, *Gleanings*, p. 326.
156. Bahá'u'lláh, *Seven Valleys*, pp. 40–1.
157. Bahá'u'lláh, *Four Valleys*, in *Seven Valleys*, pp. 53–4.
158. Bahá'u'lláh, *Gleanings*, p. 324.
159. 'Abdu'l-Bahá, *Selections*, p. 281.
160. Qur'án 96:1. Cf. Shoghi Effendi, *God Passes By*, pp. 93, 101.
161. 'Abdu'l-Bahá, *Some Answered Questions*, p. 164.
162. For references to an earlier David, see Shoghi Effendi, *Dawn of a New Day*, pp. 86–7, 93–4.
163. From a letter written on behalf of Shoghi Effendi, 28 October 1949, in *Directives of the Guardian*, p. 43.
164. See, for example, Bahá'u'lláh, *Epistle to the Son of the Wolf*, p. 117.
165. ibid. p. 57.
166. See Shoghi Effendi, *God Passes By*, p. 95.
167. Quoted in 'Abdu'l-Bahá, *Tablets of the Divine Plan*, p. 62.
168. Shoghi Effendi, *Messages to the Bahá'í World*, pp. 153–4. See the full passage for a description of another eight parts of the process.
169. Bahá'u'lláh, *Seven Valleys*, p. 4.
170. Shoghi Effendi, *God Passes By*, p. 139.
171. Shoghi Effendi, *Promised Day is Come*, p. 109.
172. From a letter written on behalf of Shoghi Effendi to an individual believer, 14 October 1935, in Shoghi Effendi, *Directives of the Guardian*, p. 40.
173. From a letter written on behalf of Shoghi Effendi to an individual believer, 31 December 1937, in *Lights of Guidance*, p. 489.
174. Shoghi Effendi, *High Endeavors*, p. 70.
175. From a letter written on behalf of Shoghi Effendi to an individual believer, 1 October 1936, in *Lights of Guidance*, p. 490.

176. From a letter written on behalf of Shoghi Effendi to an individual believer, 27 February 1938, in *Lights of Guidance*, p. 489.

177. From a letter written on behalf of Shoghi Effendi to an individual believer, 23 December 1948, in the International Bahá'í Archives.

178. Bahá'u'lláh, *Gleanings*, pp. 145–6.

179. Shoghi Effendi, *Promised Day is Come*, p. 8.

180. Shoghi Effendi, *God Passes By*, p. 100.

181. Bahá'u'lláh, quoted in Shoghi Effendi, *World Order of Bahá'u'lláh*, p. 109.

182. Bahá'u'lláh, *Gleanings*, pp. 35–6.

183. From a letter written on behalf of Shoghi Effendi, in Shoghi Effendi, *Light of Divine Guidance*, vol. 1, pp. 134–5.

184. From a letter written on behalf of Shoghi Effendi to an individual believer, 22 January 1955, in *Compilation*, vol. 2, p. 319.

185. From a letter written on behalf of Shoghi Effendi to an individual believer, 26 January 1939.

186. Bahá'u'lláh, *Gleanings*, p. 328.

187. Bahá'u'lláh, *Hidden Words*, Persian no. 19.

188. Taherzadeh, *Revelation of Bahá'u'lláh*, vol. 1, pp. 80–1.

189. Shoghi Effendi, *Unfolding Destiny*, p. 448.

190. Bahá'u'lláh, *Epistle to the Son of the Wolf*, p. 58.

191. See further references in *World Order* magazine, vol. 9, nos. 2 and 4; vol. 10, nos. 1 and 2, 'Interchange'.

192. Bahá'u'lláh, *Epistle to the Son of the Wolf*, p. 157.

193. Kitáb-i-Badí', p. 159, quoted in *World Order*, vol. 9, no. 2, p. 4.

194. Bahá'u'lláh, *Asráru'l-Athár*, vol. 4, p. 233, quoted in *World Order*, vol. 10, no. 2, p. 11.

195. *Our First Century*, cited in Sears, *Thief in the Night*, p. 194. See further details on stars and comets of the period on pp. 195–9; also Sears, *Release the Sun*, pp. 217–19.

196. Bahá'u'lláh, *Epistle to the Son of the Wolf*, p. 120. See also Nabíl, *Dawn-Breakers*, chapter 1.

197. From a letter written on behalf of Shoghi Effendi, 9 October 1947, in Shoghi Effendi, *High Endeavors*, p. 71.

198. 'Abdu'l-Bahá, *Selections*, p. 168.

199. Bahá'u'lláh, *Gleanings*, p. 298.

200. ibid. p. 105.

201. Bahá'u'lláh, *Epistle to the Son of the Wolf*, pp. 26–7.

202. Bahá'u'lláh, *Tablets*, pp. 26.
203. 'Abdu'l-Bahá, *Selections*, p. 110.
204. From a letter written on behalf of Shoghi Effendi to an individual believer, 5 August 1949, in *Living the Life*, p. 20.
205. 'Abdu'l-Bahá, *Selections*, p. 247.
206. Bahá'u'lláh, *Gleanings*, p. 105.
207. ibid. p. 49.
208. Bahá'u'lláh, *Tablets*, p. 84.
209. 'Abdu'l-Bahá, *Selections*, p. 81.
210. From a letter written on behalf of Shoghi Effendi to an individual believer, 21 February 1942.
211. 'Abdu'l-Bahá, cited in *Má'idiy-i-Ásamáni*.
212. For other references see Íqán paras. 142, 270, 272, 275, 281, 283.
213. From a letter written on behalf of Shoghi Effendi to an individual, 26 January 1939.
214. Bahá'u'lláh, *Kitáb-i-Aqdas*, para. 105.
215. Exodus 14:21.
216. Exodus 16:11–15.
217. Exodus 19: 9, 16.
218. Exodus 40: 33–8.
219. Exodus 29:45–6.
220. Exodus 3:7, 10.
221. Deuteronomy 33:2.
222. 'Abdu'l-Bahá, *Selections*, pp. 215–16.
223. Bahá'u'lláh, *Epistle to the Son of the Wolf*, p. 11.
224. ibid. p. 129.
225. 'Abdu'l-Bahá, *Selections*, pp. 167–8.
226. From a letter written on behalf of Shoghi Effendi to an individual believer, 23 February 1945, translated from the Persian.
227. Bahá'u'lláh, *Hidden Words*, Persian no. 12.
228. Bahá'u'lláh, *Gleanings*, pp. 106–7.
229. Shoghi Effendi, *High Endeavors*, p. 71.
230. Bahá'u'lláh, *Gleanings*, pp. 79–80.
231. Bahá'u'lláh, *Prayers and Meditations*, p. 194.
232. ibid. p. 283.
233. Bahá'u'lláh, *Gleanings*, p. 63.
234. ibid. p. 192 and entire section XCIV.
235. The Báb, *Selections*, p. 126.
236. Bahá'u'lláh, *Gleanings*, pp. 61–2.
237. From a letter written on behalf of Shoghi Effendi, in *High Endeavors*, p. 70.

238. Cited in Bahá'u'lláh, *Epistle to the Son of the Wolf*, p. 43.
239. Shoghi Effendi, *Unfolding Destiny*, pp. 425–6.
240. Qur'án 27:48.
241. Cited in *Bahá'í World*, vol. 13, p. 1187.
242. 'Abdu'l-Bahá, *Promulgation*, p. 295.
243. Attributed to 'Abdu'l-Bahá, in Goodall and Cooper, *Daily Lessons Received at 'Akká*, pp. 43–4.
244. From a letter written on behalf of Shoghi Effendi to a National Spiritual Assembly, 2 July 1939, in Shoghi Effendi, *Dawn of a New Day*, p. 79.
245. Bahá'u'lláh, *Epistle to the Son of the Wolf*, p. 132.
246. The Báb, *Selections*, p. 79.
247. 'Abdu'l-Bahá, in a Tablet quoted in Goodall and Cooper, *Daily Lessons Received at 'Akká*, p. 81.
248. Bahá'u'lláh, *Prayers and Meditations*, p. 42.
249. The Báb, *Selections*, p. 96.
250. Bahá'u'lláh, *Gleanings*, pp. 140–1.
251. al-Bayḍáwí.
252. Bahá'u'lláh, *Prayers and Meditations*, pp. 190–1.
253. 'Abdu'l-Bahá, in *Bahá'í World Faith*, pp. 364–5.
254. From a letter written on behalf of Shoghi Effendi to an individual believer, 30 July 1941, in *Lights of Guidance*, p. 496.
255. Cited from the Súriy-i-Damm in Bahá'u'lláh, *Gleanings*, pp. 88–90, and in Shoghi Effendi, *World Order of Bahá'u-'lláh*, pp. 118–19.
256. From a letter written on behalf of Shoghi Effendi to an individual believer, 8 February 1949), in *Lights of Guidance*, p. 498.
257. Momen, *Introduction to Shi'i Islam*, pp. 30–1.
258. *Majmú'iy-i-Alváḥ*, pp. 202–11.
259. John 19:1–16.
260. Dartmouth Bible, p. 973.
261. ibid. p. 848.
262. Bahá'u'lláh, *Tablets*, p. 10.
263. Quoted in Shoghi Effendi, *God Passes By*, p. 98.
264. Shoghi Effendi, *World Order of Bahá'u'lláh*, p. 116.
265. ibid. pp. 115–16.
266. Bahá'u'lláh, *Epistle to the Son of the Wolf*, pp.118–19.
267. Bahá'u'lláh, *Gleanings*, p. 184.
268. Bahá'u'lláh, *Prayers and Meditations*, p. 311.
269. Bahá'u'lláh, *Gleanings*, pp. 83–4.

270. Bahá'u'lláh, *Epistle to the Son of the Wolf*, p. 76.
271. See Qur'án 5:27–31 and Genesis, chapter 4.
272. Memorandum of the Research Department at the Bahá'í World Centre, 20 November 1996.
273. From a letter written on behalf of Shoghi Effendi to an individual believer, 8 February 1949, in *Lights of Guidance*, p. 498.
274. Bahá'u'lláh, *Gleanings*, p. 101.
275. Bahá'u'lláh, *Prayers and Meditations*, p. 54.
276. Bahá'u'lláh, *Gleanings*, p. 183.
277. ibid. pp. 197–8.
278. From a letter written on behalf of Shoghi Effendi to an individual believer, 14 March 1955, in *Lights of Guidance*, p. 478.
279. The Báb, *Selections*, pp. 105–6.
280. See Shoghi Effendi, *God Passes By*, p. 347.
281. Al Beidawi, Jallaloddin, Al Zamakh.
282. From a letter written on behalf of Shoghi Effendi to an individual believer, 13 December 1948.
283. Shoghi Effendi, *God Passes By*, p. 214. See also Bahá'u'lláh, *Tablets*, I<u>sh</u>ráqát, pp. 108–10; and 'Abdu'l-Bahá, *Some Answered Questions*, p. 171.
284. Bahá'u'lláh, *Kitáb-i-Aqdas*, para. 161. Also at Bahá'u'lláh, *Gleanings*, pp. 86–7.
285. 'Abdu'l-Bahá, *Tablets*, vol. 2, p. 244.
286. Attributed to 'Abdu'l-Bahá, in *Star of the West*, vol. 8, no. 11, p. 143.
287. Bahá'u'lláh, *Epistle to the Son of the Wolf*, p. 41.
288. Bahá'u'lláh, quoted in Shoghi Effendi, *World Order of Bahá'u'lláh*, p. 113.
289. ibid. p. 114.
290. Bahá'u'lláh, *Epistle to the Son of the Wolf*, p. 42–3.
291. From a letter written on behalf of Shoghi Effendi to an individual believer, 2 November 1938.
292. From a letter written on behalf of Shoghi Effendi to an individual believer, 19 April 1947, in *Lights of Guidance*, p. 475.
293. From a letter written on behalf of Shoghi Effendi to an individual believer, 4 October 1950, Shoghi Effendi, *Unfolding Destiny*, pp. 457–8.
294. 'Abdu'l-Bahá, *Selections*, p. 207.
295. Bahá'u'lláh, *Hidden Words*, Persian no. 3.
296. Shoghi Effendi, *Dawn of a New Day*, p. 200.

290 A COMPANION TO THE STUDY OF THE KITÁB-I-ÍQÁN

297. From a letter written on behalf of Shoghi Effendi to two believers, 7 December 1935, in *Lights of Guidance*, p. 482.
298. From a letter written on behalf of Shoghi Effendi to an individual believer, 29 October 1938, in Shoghi Effendi, *Dawn of a New Day*, p. 202.
299. From a letter written on behalf of Shoghi Effendi to an individual believer, August 1936, in Shoghi Effendi, *Directives of the Guardian*, pp. 7–8.
300. Shoghi Effendi, *God Passes By*, pp. 24–5.
301. Shoghi Effendi, *Promised Day is Come*, p. 25.
302. Shoghi Effendi, *World Order of Bahá'u'lláh*, p. 102.
303. Bahá'u'lláh, *Tablets*, pp. 87, 89.
304. Shoghi Effendi, *God Passes By*, p. 50.
305. ibid. pp. 11–12; see also pp. 42–4, 50.
306. ibid. p. 12. See also pp. 44 and 50.
307. ibid. p. 10.
308. Bahá'u'lláh, *Gleanings*, p. 63.
309. Shoghi Effendi, *God Passes By*, p. 27.
310. Nabíl, *Dawn-Breakers*, pp. 304–5.
311. Shoghi Effendi, *God Passes By*, p. 23.
312. ibid. p. 54.
313. ibid. p. 51.
314. Bahá'u'lláh, *Gleanings*, p. 146.
315. Shoghi Effendi, *World Order of Bahá'u'lláh*, p. 123.
316. Shoghi Effendi, *God Passes By*, p. 25.
317. From a letter written on behalf of Shoghi Effendi to an individual believer, 10 July 1939, in *Lights of Guidance*, p. 483.
318. From a letter written on behalf of Shoghi Effendi to an individual believer, 16 January 1939.
319. Shoghi Effendi, *God Passes By*, p. 91.
320. ibid. p. 118.
321. The Báb, *Selections*, p. 12.
322. Bahá'u'lláh, quoted in Shoghi Effendi, *World Order of Bahá'u'lláh*, p. 104.
323. See Qur'án 5:27–31; also Genesis, chapter 4.
324. See Qur'án 11.
325. See Shoghi Effendi, *God Passes By*, p. 91.
326. See Bahá'u'lláh, *Epistle to the Son of the Wolf*, p. 112.
327. Qur'án 27:48. Also referred to at 33:6.
328. Qur'án 20:85.
329. Shoghi Effendi, *Bahá'í Administration*, p. 185.

330. Shoghi Effendi, *World Order of Bahá'u'lláh*, p. 58.
331. ibid. p. 102.
332. ibid. p. 114.
333. ibid. p. 115.
334. ibid. p. 118.
335. Shoghi Effendi, *Promised Day is Come*, p. 108.
336. Shoghi Effendi, *God Passes By*, p. 100.
337. Shoghi Effendi, Statement to the United Nations Commission on Palestine, 1947, in *Promised Day is Come*, p. v.